Thinking at Every Desk

Thinking at Every Desk

Four Simple Skills
to Transform Your Classroom

Derek Cabrera
Laura Colosi

W. W. Norton & Company
New York • London

Copyright © 2012, 2009 by Derek Cabrera and Laura Colosi

For information about permission to reproduce selections from this book, write to Permissions, W. W. Norton & Company, Inc., 500 Fifth Avenue, New York, NY 10110

For information about special discounts for bulk purchases, please contact W. W. Norton Special Sales at specialsales@wwnorton.com or 800-233-4830

Manufacturing by Quad Graphics Fairfield
Book design by Ken Gross
Production manager: Leeann Graham

Library of Congress Cataloging-in-Publication Data

Cabrera, Derek, author.
    Thinking at every desk : four simple skills to transform your classroom / Derek Cabrera, Laura Colosi.
        pages   cm. — (Norton books in education)
    Includes bibliographical references and index.
    ISBN 978-0-393-70756-4 (pbk.)
    1. Effective teaching. 2. Critical thinking. I. Colosi, Laura, author. II. Title.
    LB1025.3.C325 2012
    371.102—dc23   2012015978

ISBN: 978-0-393-70756-4 (pbk.)

W. W. Norton & Company, Inc., 500 Fifth Avenue, New York, N.Y. 10110
www.wwnorton.com
W. W. Norton & Company Ltd., Castle House, 75/76 Wells Street, London W1T 3QT

1 2 3 4 5 6 7 8 9 0

In memory of my father, Eduardo Cabrera, the greatest teacher I have ever known. And to our three children, Elena, Gianna, and Carter.

Contents

Acknowledgments

t's cliche to say that there are too many people to thank, but it's true. There are too many people to thank. When you are lucky enough, like we have been, to be involved in so many districts and schools and classrooms and to meet so many inspiring administrators, principals, teachers, and students, it is difficult to create a list of all the people who deserve praise. Most of all we want to thank the many teachers who have taken it upon themselves to bring thinking to those students in their care. We want to thank our editors at W.W. Norton, our mentors and colleagues at Cornell University among other universities, and of course, our families who have supported us in all of our endeavors. We also must mention the many educators who have helped us make an idea into a movement for social and educational change.

Maura Burke	Shani Brown	Harold Closter
Ann Erickson	Jennifer Orr	Cristy Nowak
Mary Ann Ryan	Betsi Closter	Karen Davis
Meghan Callahan	Polly Dredge	Brenda Delaney
Edithe Dobbins Jordan	Lenor Cummings	Lori Sakauye
Jesse Kraft	Debra Porter	Lauren Shernoff
Debby Fulcher	Christina Dickens	Cindy Sweeder
Peter Noonan	Josie Mani	Barbara Havens

Joe Lacey
Kerry Ickrath
Susan Anselene
Susan Martin
Janet Molan
George Towery
Eileen Delaney
June Hiller
Mark Smith
Ann Monday
Carol Horn
Alan Borhauer
Cynthia Lowry
Michelle Kem
Shannon Philips
  Maxson
Erin Martindale
Jessica Stratton
Heather Byrne
Christa Salmon
Dawn Blanchard
LeAnn Sinclair
Jaime Saroka
Dee Hart
Kathy Baumgardner
Donna Stagner
Jennifer Malone
Drenon Fite
John Nittolo

Kim Metcalf
  Permenter
Louis Rossi
Lee Kaltman
Lee Ginenthal
Jerry Christy
Tracy Kahn
George Ness
Cindy Young
Deborah Knapp
Gary Nuss
Bill Martens
Cori Cotner
Carol Fontaine
Chad Devoe
Dave Cooper
Boris Simkin
Will Provine
Rosemary Caffarella
Raymond Wlodkowski
Jerry Ziegler
Deborah Hoard
Che Broadnax
Lee Fritz
Amy Saxton
Peter Mason
Scott and Yvonne
  Campbell
Kathy Howlett

Bruce Howlett
Antonia Rudenstine
Claire Lobdell
Ginger Richardson
Michelle Bloodworth
Carlos Romero
Susan Stivers
Marianna O'Brien
Leighton Arnold
Jennifer Kushner
Mike O'Neill
Byungho Son
Amy Minor
David Perrigo
Chris Cabrera
Ruth Cabrera
Brian Cabrera
Sonia Cabrera
Sabrina Hill
Gianna Colosi
Elena Colosi
Dottie Crago
Walter Faust
NS Liu
Dasaratha Rama
Benjamin Hunt
Cindy Langdon
Ling Hua Loon
Wong Mui Chong

Preface

M y family dinner table was my alma mater. It's the place where I
learned to love the pursuit of knowledge. It's the place where
I learned to think. My mother's only hard and fast rule was that
we all had to be at dinner every night. Each night we talked about everything under the sun, from the silly to the serious: what we did at school
that day, squabbles with my siblings, current events, politics, science, reli-
gion, anything.

We played with our food; in fact, we were encouraged to do so. My
father had a strange habit of using anything on the table—food, salt and
pepper shakers, forks, knives, napkins, and even the plates—to represent
any idea he was explaining in whatever topic we were discussing.

"Dad, what do they mean by Reaganomics?"

"Reaganomics is a portmanteau," he'd say, "a word that fuses Presi-
dent Reagan and economics," squishing two chunks of soft bread together.
Then he shaped the new piece of bread into a bowl and held it out for us
to see. He continued: "Reaganomics has four key components." He then
dropped a piece of diced chicken into the bread bowl as he listed each one:
"Reduction of government spending, regulation, taxation, and inflation."
And so it continued.

"Dad, what's regulation mean?"

"Well, if you take this large spoon and this small spoon and scoop rice from the bowl, you'll see that the structure of the spoon—its size—regulates the amount of rice that . . ."

And so it went every night at dinnertime.

These early experiences had a great effect on me. First, it became virtually impossible for me to eat at my friends' houses. More important, adopting my father's habit of explaining concepts gave me an eye, a feel, and a love for ideas that led me to the formal study of how we create them. I could actually see the ideas on the table, in literal form. They were no longer entangled in my head—they were right on the table in front of me. I could hold any idea (in the form of a piece of a bread) in my hand, manipulate it, move it around, and combine it with others. I could take an idea from my brother, change it, add or subtract from it, and hand it back to him. Ideas were literally and figuratively tangible.

I loved ideas and how adventurous they could be: They were to be played with, constructed, combined, interrelated, explored. The world of ideas became my favorite playground. Knowledge became my muse. While other kids built skyscrapers and dinosaurs, I built ideas. I became fascinated early on with how ideas are made and how we can share them with others—this led to more than 15 years of formal research into the process of constructing ideas among any and all learners. This process is the crux of education.

My father taught me how to construct and deconstruct knowledge. I learned to distinguish and differentiate ideas, to break ideas into parts or merge them into wholes, to make connections between and among ideas, and to consider things from different points of view. In short, I learned how to think.

In this book, my colleague Laura Colosi and I explain the implications of my research into thinking (cognition), thinking about thinking (metacognition), and the teaching of thinking (pedagogy). You will learn some of what we've learned about how thinking works—and how thinking skills can be taught—as the result of our understanding of how knowledge is structured.

—Derek Cabrera

CHAPTER ONE

Introduction
Thinking at Every Desk

W hen Derek first began to teach at an Ivy League university, he had high hopes. After all, the kids who get into institutions like Harvard, Oxford, MIT, Cornell, Stanford, and Princeton are the students who did everything right in the K-12 educational system. They did their homework, received good grades, studied for tests, took as many AP courses as possible, enrolled in extracurriculars, and fastidiously obeyed the many instructions we gave them from preschool until 12th grade.

These kids were the cream of the crop. The best of the best. The poster children for our American educational system. They were star students, and they were rewarded with admittance into the most prestigious schools. And now Derek was a faculty member at one of these prestigious schools, so naturally, he had high expectations of his students' abilities. It wasn't long into his first year of teaching that he noticed something he didn't expect. His students couldn't think critically. Their "wildly successful" K-12 experience had actually compromised this ability. An educator, Sir Ken Robinson, has said that our schools are killing the art of creative thinking. This is true. But he doesn't go far enough. Our schools are not just killing creativity. The training that kids are receiving in school is also killing several different and important kinds of thinking that students desperately need throughout their lives:

- **Critical thinking:** Being analytical and logical in framing problems.
- **Creative thinking:** Thinking differently and outside the box in order to address tough, interconnected problems.
- **Interdisciplinary thinking:** Interrelating what they learn in breadth and depth. Problems don't respect disciplinary boundaries, and neither will the needed solutions.
- **Scientific thinking:** Using their capacity and skills to question, analyze, be methodological, and build on prior knowledge and use information to address problems formally.
- **Systems thinking:** Understanding the interconnectedness of systems, concentric circles of context, and unintended consequences.
- **Prosocial thinking (emotional intelligence):** Working in teams to solve the most pressing problems; talking, listening, and collaborating with others to resolve problems, distinguish between thoughts and feelings, and keep their egos in check.

Derek had wondered about his students. If they weren't learning to think, what had they been learning during all those years of "successful" schooling? What they learned soon became clear. First, they learned to memorize a tremendous amount of information with great efficiency. They were full of facts, many of them encyclopedically so. Yet, while they were chock-a-block with information, they lacked the knowledge for how to get things done. They lacked the know-how to adapt what they knew and use it in novel situations. Among his students, few of them could use information for any useful purpose other than regurgitating it on a test. They were information-*full* but not knowledge-*able*.

Second, through painstaking attention to detail, they had become good at school. Being naturally smart, they had figured out at a relatively early age the simple pattern of how to pass classes in school and had mastered it. Most of them had mastered it so thoroughly that they could achieve straight A's with a minimum amount of effort. They were good at "doing school." But does that translate into being good at life? Derek's students could pass any test he gave them as long as it followed the basic instructional approach they had become familiar with since somewhere around the third grade: A teacher reviews the information that is going to be on the test and then students memorize and provide the same facts on test day. Sadly, that is how his students, and hundreds of thousands of others in the United States, define "learning." Nothing could be further from the truth.

If his students were ever to be game show contestants on *Jeopardy*, they were well prepared to succeed. But they were not prepared for the real challenges of life: challenges that would require them to be knowledge-able, not merely information-full.

You might think that this is an education problem because it starts with how we teach our young. It is actually a serious social and economic problem—and the tentacles of this problem reach into and wreak havoc on every part of our society. Whether it is the Ivy League or the many other great institutions that dot the landscape, our K–12 system is not adequately preparing future generations for the challenges of life in demanding times. Our country deserves a better system. Our children deserve to be better prepared.

So, what's going on? How could this happen? How could these students be at this point in their academic achievement and have so little real-life skills to speak of? It saddened us when we realized that these were the kids who did absolutely everything we told them to do. As you will see, they were not the problem. The poet Robert Frost wrote, "Two roads diverged in a wood, and I—I took the one less traveled by / And that has made all the difference." We told them to go the wrong way! They have not taken the road that makes all the difference. What is the different path from the usual trajectory of a student who becomes merely information-*full*? Where is the path by which the student will end up being knowledge-*able*? Let's take a look at where we steered them wrong and how we can fix this catastrophic problem we all face.

We can begin by understanding information. What is information? Information is content: the curriculum, the standards, the subject matter. It is the "stuff" we teach. If we wanted to end up with students who are information-full, the educational process should focus on the instruction and memorization of information. And, that's exactly what we do in education (with few exceptions). Remember the "rules of the game" that students learned early in their educational career:

Rule #1: The teacher instructs information that will be on the test.

Rule #2: The students memorize information.

Rule #3: The students take a test.

Rule #4: Voila! Learning occurred.

Follow these rules over and over again and you'll get college students who are information-full. If that's what you want, that's the path and don't deviate from it.

But, of course, that's not what we want. We want knowledgeable kids who are not only good at school but good at living life. Kids should think creatively, critically, and independently. What are the rules of the game that lead to knowledgeable kids? Where is their path? What's the magic ingredient? Thinking. Thinking is the not-so-magic ingredient that, as Mr. Frost said, makes all the difference. Rather than memorizing and recalling information, students must structure and create information. When they structure information, they build knowledge. When they memorize information, they retain information. That's the difference that will make all the difference.

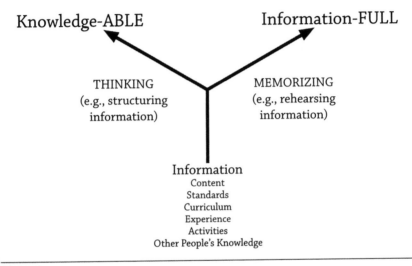

Knowledge-ABLE

Information-FULL

THINKING
(e.g., structuring
information)

MEMORIZING
(e.g., rehearsing
information)

Information
Content
Standards
Curriculum
Experience
Activities
Other People's Knowledge

Figure 1

If we look a little deeper at Figure 1, we can see a profoundly important and universal equation for education itself. A map, if you will, for ensuring that students become knowledgeable, not just information-full. The road less traveled—the one to the left—is where information and thinking lead to knowledge.

Knowledge = Information x Thinking

Let's review what these three terms mean in order to distinguish them from each other. Information is content, the standards of learning, facts, the curriculum, even experiences and activities (and, in a twist that is slightly more complex, even other people's knowledge is information because we are the only ones who can build knowledge for ourselves; we can't get it from someone else). That's information. As a teacher, the curriculum is what we mean when we say information.

So, what is knowledge? Knowledge is actionable information: It is information you can use to solve a problem, navigate a situation, or figure something out. Knowledge is the way we use information and how we activate it. In fact, if we think of thinking as being synonymous with structuring information in meaningful ways, then the equation tells us exactly what knowledge is—information multiplied by thinking.

$$K = I \times T$$

So, where did we go wrong? When did we begin to lead our students astray? It happened when we left out the "T" in the equation. We made the mistake that Knowledge and Information were the same. That is, we made the mistake that $K = I$. However, they are not the same thing: $K \neq I$.

As educators, we focused on only the content curriculum (all the stuff we teach). We assumed that if we just covered the curriculum, everything would work out in the end. We gave the content absolute power. We made it king. Over time, though, the Content King became tyrannical. Today, it lauds its control over all of us. The content curriculum (information) is not just important. It is very important. In fact, it is half the equation, and you need information to make knowledge. But information is not the same thing as knowledge. If you're looking for the root cause of why things are the way they are in education today and if you are looking for the underlying reasons why students get to college full of facts but short of knowledge, it is because we dropped the T from the equation for education.

Do you want to know how it happened? It happened slowly, incrementally over time. It happened through tiny lessons taught all across the globe. These lessons between teacher and student focused on the erroneous belief that $K = I$ and left off the T. Derek will often have lunch with colleagues, many of whom are faculty in the physical sciences (physics, chemistry, etc.). Inevitably they'll bring up their classes (which many research scientists don't like very much because they believe it distracts them from their research). Derek likes to poke a bit of fun at them about their teaching methods. Here's how the conversation usually goes:

Colleague: I gotta run and teach my class.
Derek: You don't teach, do you?
Colleague: Of course I do, I have a class at 1:30. You know that. . . .

Derek: Oh, right. But you don't teach, do you? You just walk in and know in front of people.

That gets them every time. And it points out a very important idea. We think that if we are in front of people knowing, talking, sharing our knowledge that that is teaching. It is not. We think that if we are teaching, then they are learning. But nothing could be further from the truth. In fact, the great educational philosopher Paulo Freire said, "There is no teaching without learning." What he meant by that is that the only way to determine if there is teaching occurring is if learning is occurring. Learning tells us that teaching occurred, not the other way around. Teaching is not the same as knowing in front of people or talking in front of a room. Although during the teaching process, we might talk in front of the room and know in front of our students, teaching is the process by which we ensure that learning is occurring by understanding what is being constructed in our students' minds. Ideally, our students build the same knowledge as what we are spewing, but that is often not the case. They may be building knowledge—constructing ideas—that have little to do with what is being taught. In high school chemistry when Derek's teacher discussed the dynamics of molecules, he thought about social dynamics and how it seemed similar because that was the most relevant thing he wanted to understand during the social tumult of high school. The chemistry teacher wasn't teaching social dynamics, but that's what Derek was learning.

Here is a thought experiment. Imagine that all of your students show up one day wearing white T-shirts with large black letters that read "Awaiting Instructions." How would you approach these students? What would you do to prepare to teach them today? The next day, all of your students are wearing shirts that read "Under Construction." How would you now approach these students? What would you do to prepare to teach them today?

We've presented these scenarios to educators across the country. "Awaiting Instructions" conjures up a classroom, with a teacher stationed at the front of the room, the "sage on the stage," leading a lesson through talk and demonstration. The students act as sponges, absorbing the information as the teacher pours it out. This implies a one-way relationship between the teacher and student that is reliant in the teacher's presentation of information to the student. Information is fixed, static, and there are right and wrong answers.

In contrast, "Under Construction" conjures up a classroom full of students who are actively engaged in lessons, perhaps through hands-on

| *Figure 2* | *Figure 3* |

stations or small-group work, led by a "guide on the side" teacher whose questions are open-ended, and who questions the students frequently. The relationship between the teacher and students is based on the dynamic interactions among them—and, more important, on the students' ability to build their knowledge based on the teacher's expressed goal of any lesson. Constructing knowledge allows for the "right" answer, which is often found in a sea of other valid or plausible answers.

The crucial point of this exercise is that, regardless of whether the teacher acts as a "sage on the stage" or a "guide on the side," students will construct their knowledge in *both* situations. All students are constructivists. The human brain is constructivist. This fact does not change based on the classroom setting or teacher's practice. Yet, today, the most popular educational paradigm is not constructivism but instructionism. When we say popular, we mean there is no contest. The vast overwhelming majority of schools in this country and throughout the world are built upon the foundations of instructionism. Instructionism is a simple idea. It simply says that students can get knowledge. We can put knowledge into them. In effect, instructionism says that $K = I$.

Instructionism is wildly seductive because it's a powerful idea due to its massive efficiency and simple premise. The basic idea is best explained with the analogy that people are like computers. In the same way that we can transfer a Word file from one computer to another, we can take some knowledge that exists in one person (a teacher or expert) and download it into the head of another person (the student). The idea is so efficient because it means that it is possible to stand in front of a room knowing things in front of people and that that knowledge will somehow get into the students' heads. It makes little difference how many students are in the room. As long as they are tuned in and paying attention, then the knowledge will pour into their heads. What's even better about instructionism is that once the knowledge has been deposited into the students' heads, we can assess whether it got into their heads by testing. The idea is a bit like running the search function on a hard drive. If you search for a particular file or folder, then hit the Enter button, voila! It is located and we know that learning has occurred.

Look at what we do today in education and you will see a system that believes this to be true about how humans learn. Of course, for all of its powerful efficiency and assessability, instructionism does have one tiny little flaw. It is not real. It has nothing to do with how humans learn. Students never simply absorb what is being instructed. Scholars and educators once commonly accepted that knowledge could be moved from one person (a teacher or expert) to another (a student or novice). This is simply not true. What actually happens is your students interpret everything they hear, see, or touch in relation to their prior knowledge and experiences, and they transform what they're taught into new knowledge through the process of thinking.

Our practice is always a good indication of what we believe. Thus, based on what occurs in our schools you would have to conclude that (1) any lesson can simply be put into a kid's head and (2) the relationship between knowledge and thinking is tenuous at best. Yet, the truth is that kids cannot "get" knowledge, they have to build it. And the relationship between knowledge and thinking is not tenuous, it's nonnegotiable. Knowledge and thinking exist in an endless cycle. They coexist in a feedback loop in which the process of thinking creates the product of knowledge. This knowledge informs further thinking, which creates new knowledge. This is why other people's knowledge comes to us as information. In order to know it, we have to build it ourselves.

Our teaching methods still haven't caught up to this fact. Even the advent of interactive technologies does not move teaching toward a constructivist approach, and it does not develop the higher-order thinking skills that are at the forefront of the current educational wish list. For example, if a student sits passively through a traditional college lecture, takes notes on salient points for the test, takes the test and then passes it, they have recalled the content curriculum—the information—but nothing more.

Now let's take that same lesson but this time the students have handheld PDA devices that periodically ask students to answer multiple-choice questions. Their collective answers are presented to them on the board (as feedback). In this situation, the teacher has increased interaction and engagement through technology, but the pedagogy is still instructivism. The students do not demonstrate the knowledge they built, only the highly structured answers to highly structured questions. Students know exactly how to run this prestructured maze to get the piece of cheese with the least effort. The teacher does not create activities that elucidate how students built the knowledge they are learning. Whether this example occurs in a classroom setting or online by using technology is irrelevant to the point. The inclusion of technology in a classroom does not mean that students are thinking more deeply about the lesson content, nor does it illustrate higher use of thinking skills or understanding of one's thinking processes—what it demonstrates is that students are proficient with technology.

Classroom practices should require students to think about how they are constructing knowledge. For example, students need to look at a particular topic from two or more different perspectives. This helps students to understand not only the topic being studied but also a meta-level skill of taking a perspective that can be used in other lessons or topics. Likewise, students need different ways to organize, sort, and group (all part/whole) various ideas. For example, they can create a meaning map of a book.

It is not constructivist if the lesson does not require students to build knowledge and understand how they built it. When we think, we build knowledge. When we use someone else's hard-won knowledge, we do not receive it as knowledge; it comes to us as information. We then use thinking to process that information into actionable knowledge. We, and by we, we mean all living humans, do not get knowledge, we build it.

Yet we cling to our instructionist foundations because we want so badly for it to be true. We want to believe in the unicorn of instructionism. It makes life easy. It makes teaching easy. It makes knowing easy. It makes us feel happy because we are in control. We like our information—our facts—to be clean, testable using multiple-choice and true-false questions. We don't want to hear bubkes about knowledge changing all the time and how messy it really is to construct knowledge. We are happy in our little instructivist cocoons. Leave us alone, thank you. We're happy, that is, until we see that our students have made it to college and cannot think. Then it's a real drag.

We like our facts like we like our chicken. Think about it. When you go to the chicken aisle at the supermarket you have some expectations. You expect your chicken to be clean, neat, tidy. You expect plump packets of equal sized, pink flesh. A date that says the meat is fresh. You expect the little sponge underneath, the plastic wrap, the freshness seal. Most important, you expect that your chicken will not resemble, in any way, shape, and form, a chicken. You don't want feathers and bones. No veins. No blood. No beaks or feet. We like our facts the same way. We like the information that we use in the content curriculum of schools to be sterilized from the real, messy process of building knowledge. We want our facts to be clean. We especially like our facts to remain true, that is, to never change. Indeed, most students believe that facts don't change, because we teach facts as if they don't change. Nothing could be further from the truth. Facts are constantly changing as new knowledge is built.

Again, our practice belies our beliefs and desires that knowledge should remain static and reliable. We memorize the planets of our solar system; we explore the biology of species; we teach the five senses, and on and on. We teach all sorts of facts like they're diamonds that will shine forever. In truth, knowledge is constantly changing in three important ways: growth, validity, and relevancy.

The quantity of knowledge grows and expands simply because of the first law: Everyone is constantly building new knowledge. In the realm of scientific knowledge, we've gone from a handful of disciplines (e.g., physics, chemistry, psychology) to more than 20,000 disciplines and subfields at last count (e.g., biochemistry, genomics, ichthyology, enology). Today, there are 338 different "ologies," or areas of scientific study. There are more than 300,000 scientific journals and periodicals. We're inundated with information. For example, it's estimated that there are 540,000 words in the English language today. This is five times more than the number of words that existed during Shakespeare's lifetime. Today, many academic disciplines are growing so quickly that scholars cannot keep up with everything in their field, and areas of specialization emerge more and more in disciplines.

Facts are neither timeless nor static. Humans learn new things all the time, and as new knowledge comes in, the validity of previously established facts changes. Pluto was a planet. The Earth was flat. African Americans were genetically inferior to whites. Animals didn't use tools, and on and on. One fact that will never change is that octopi have eight legs. That's because the word "octopus" literally means "eight-footed." So it's a no-brainer that they have eight legs, right? Right? Wrong. Researchers studying Mavis, a giant Pacific octopus, and Olga, a common octopus, were surprised to find that their most basic assumptions were wrong. In data collected from more than 2,000 observations, when Mavis and Olga played with a variety of toys, including a Rubik's Cube, the octopi—to everyone's surprise—used six of their eight appendages more like arms, and the remaining two functioned like legs!* The facts change over time. Legs become arms, planets become dwarfs, there's even debate about what caused the mass extinction of the dinosaurs . . . stay tuned.

Kids have a knack for finding the one thing that's sure to drive adults nuts. When Derek was a teenager, the irritant was skateboarding. (Today, it might be video gaming or texting.) Avid skateboarders attacked this emerging area of knowledge with all the vim and vigor of new scientists: They distinguished among different tricks; developed new methods of skating, such as empty pools, ramps, freestyle, and street curbs; and even researched new materials that could be used for softer wheels, better decks and trucks, and skate clothing and shoes. They took to empty pools (and to emptying pools!) so they could develop new "rad" tricks. They turned parks and sidewalks into makeshift skate parks. They raided building sites for scraps of lumber and sheets of plywood to build half- and even full-pipe ramps. The school's wood-shop class became popular because skateboarders needed woodworking skills to make custom decks and ramps.

In response to all of this, adults—teachers, school administrators, city planners, parents, mayors, and the police—vehemently objected. As skateboarding grew in popularity, so did the official response in the form of prohibition. New no-skateboarding policies sprung up in schools, and no-skating ordinances were posted in city parks and downtown areas. Boards were confiscated, making the wood shop all the more popular. The overarching reason that adults gave for the crackdown was that skateboarding was irrelevant. Skaters should be studying something more useful. Skateboarding would not amount to anything and was irrelevant knowledge.

Of course, it did amount to something. At the 1999 X Games, with more than 275,000 people in attendance, a young skater named Tony Hawk executed the first 900—a 900-degree spin considered to be one of skateboarding's most difficult and elusive tricks. Today, Tony Hawk has his very own skater doll, which can be purchased at any number of stores, alongside his line of video games on PlayStation and Xbox. The skateboarding craze and the extreme alternative sports industry it helped to spawn have not

---

*From "How many arms does an octopus have? Only six—the other two are legs, say scientists." *Daily Mail Reporter*, 13 August 2008.

merely provided an arena for a few talented athletes. They have spawned a mega-industry, producing anything from cars and clothing to food and beverages, not to mention opportunities for iconoclastic commentary, stage setup, and countless other jobs. The skeptics were wrong when they predicted skateboarding knowledge would be irrelevant. Those who are passionate and know something about skateboarding no longer seem so misguided.

Bodies of knowledge are constantly growing and changing in validity and relevancy. When we teach students the facts of today, we must also remind ourselves that today's facts are part of a larger territory that is always expanding. We want our students to constantly look for such growths in knowledge, to be lifelong seekers of new knowledge, and to develop the ability to significantly contribute to our collective bodies of knowledge as well. Additionally, if we know how knowledge is constructed, and that it is changing, as educators we should seek to understand *how* it is constructed and to know the ways in which it is changing. Students need to know stuff, but they also need to know *how* they know stuff. If we continue to focus on *what* stuff students need to know at the expense of *how* to know stuff, they will drown in the ever-expanding sea of information. Knowing both *what* they know and *how* they know it allows them to approach any new topic or situation in life with great proficiency and metacognition: They will be lifelong learners who possess both competence and confidence.

Scientists have a name for the field of study of how knowledge changes. It is called "evolutionary epistemology." That's a mouthful but it's easy to break down into its two parts. "Evolutionary" simply means change over time and "epistemology" means the study of knowledge. So the whole term means that knowledge changes over time. Whether you like the slightly pedantic term or not, you'll likely appreciate some of the synonyms of evolutionary epistemology:

- Creativity
- Innovation
- Invention
- Science
- Progress

If knowledge didn't change and if, as we like to pretend in our schools, knowledge stayed the same, we wouldn't have creativity, innovation, invention, science, and progress. We wouldn't have iPhones, the Internet, and Hubble photos of Jupiter or Mars. Instead, we'd be stuck in the past, clinging to our outdated, but clean and simple, facts.

I've often said that there should be a Nobel Prize given for the noble science of education—teaching and learning. It would have such a remarkable impact on our field by encouraging people to innovate and dig deeper into the art and science of pedagogy or to explore and find the universal laws that govern all human learning. Of course, there isn't a Nobel Prize for education. There is one example of an educator being recognized at a high level. One of *Time* Magazine's "100 Greatest Minds of the Century" was an educator: Jean Piaget. Piaget had a lot of ideas but only one of his ideas got him on this list with the other 99 sharpest minds of the last century. Einstein, a contemporary of Piaget's, commented on Piaget and his idea. He said, "Piaget's idea was so simple only a genius could have thought of it."

What was the single idea that saw an educator rise to a level so rarely achieved? It must be an idea that every teacher and educator should pay close attention to. Piaget's idea was constructivism. At its core, it was the simple idea that K = I x T. We need to structure our information in order to make it useable and in order to make it into knowledge.

Constructivism and evolutionary epistemology, as research-based practices, create an interesting dilemma for our schools. If what we teach today may change over time, even become invalid or irrelevant, what will our students do as they enter the real world? What will people need to survive in a world where many of the facts they've learned don't survive and the only way to "get" new knowledge is to think? The answer is simple. We must equip our students to approach any new knowledge by teaching them not only what to know (content knowledge) but also how to know (thinking skills). Content knowledge and thinking skills must be taught in balance. Yet again, when we look at our schools, we see a dangerous imbalance. We see a mismatch between our practices and reality.

- We see a system that behaves as if students can "get" knowledge and teachers can "give" it. However, we know that knowledge is built.
- We see a system that behaves as if facts are static and reliable forever. However, knowledge is constantly changing.
- We see a system that behaves as if knowledge and information are the same thing, yet we know that information and thinking lead to knowledge.

In sum, our schools use an Industrial Age mind-set to train students for the Knowledge Age. If we continue on this path, every American child will be left behind. Perhaps most important today, thinking skills are viewed as crucial for educated persons to cope with a rapidly changing world. Many educators believe that specific knowledge of facts will not be as important to tomorrow's workers and citizens as will be the ability to learn and make sense of new information.*

We need citizens who not only possess information but can also think—that is, people who can use the information to create new knowledge and solve novel problems. Yet, by both commission (overemphasizing content-based curriculum) and by omission (failing to teach them thinking skills), we're letting our students down. Our current situation is a call to action for educators. We must develop both content knowledge and robust thinking skills in every student. Instead, we focus almost entirely on content knowledge, testing, memorization, and recall.

Ole Kirk Christiansen, a carpenter, founded Lego in 1932. At the time, he was out of work because of the Depression and he decided to build wooden toys (piggy banks, etc.) in Denmark. In 1947 Ole got samples of a plastic brick invented and patented ("self-locking building bricks") by Mr. Hilary "Harry" Fisher Page in Britain, and he began creating the automatic binding bricks that we know today as Lego Bricks, a name that originated in 1953. Today, Lego, with its headquarters in Billund, Denmark, is the sixth largest toy company in the world, with over 5,000 employees and revenue of $7.8 billion Danish Kroner.

When we were kids, Lego Building Bricks came in a big bucket. You could build anything! In fact, Ole's 1958 Lego patent 3005282 states, "The principle object of the invention is to provide for a vast variety of combinations of the bricks for making toy structures of many different kinds and shapes." And that was the magic of Lego. Anything you could imagine, you could build. Every kid could unleash his creativity on the world. Children today may never know the joy of unbridled creativity. Licensing has become one of the toy industry's most lucrative venues, and Lego is no exception. Inundated with over 130 new licensed Lego kits per year, children can choose among works that are connected to the worlds of Thomas and Friends, Bob the Builder, Batman, Star Wars, Indiana Jones, and SpongeBob SquarePants. Each kit is guided by step-by-step instructions, using the same amount of creativity needed to read a VCR manual.

---

*Wolf, Edward N. (2005, October). The growth of information workers in the U.S. economy, 1950–2000: The role of technological change, computerization, and structural change. *Communications of the ACM*, 48(10), 37–42.

In contrast to the unbounded play mentioned in the original patent, these licensed kits only allow children to build predesigned structures.

This is not to say that Lego's new licensed products lack creativity. Indeed, the designer's desks at Lego's headquarters are teeming with creative ideas. Perhaps for profit or consumer demand Lego has changed its business strategy, but the net effect for children around the world is that what was once open to imagination is now closed by instruction. The physical construction is now scripted, robbing children of the cognitive construction that was once the point. The result is that the creativity and construction that once filled the hands and minds of children everywhere is now being written into directions at a corporate desk in Denmark.

Here's our fear. Educators, teachers, curriculum designers, and others—all with the best of intentions—acting similarly in preparing content for classroom consumption. They are surgically removing the messy constructions and the possibility for learning from mistakes. Thinking happens, but it happens at the wrong desk. It needs to happen at the student's desk. The Lego story serves as a poignant reminder to curriculum designers and teachers everywhere: When we overprepare for the class, we are robbing our students of the opportunity to build their own ideas. We must insure that the construction happens at the right desk, not the teacher's or curriculum designer's desk. Without thinking at every desk, your students will not be invited to sit at the knowledge tables of the future. In a nutshell, we need to put the T for Thinking back into the educational equation. We took it out some time ago in order to prepare our students to work in factories. But, if you haven't noticed, the United States doesn't have many factories left and there's a high probability that students won't be working on assembly lines.

In all our travels across the United States and abroad, we've never met an educator who authentically disagrees with the importance of thinking skills. We've never met a teacher, principal, or administrator who is anti-thinking. What we have seen are a lot of teachers, principals, and administrators who don't know how to get the T back into the curriculum. We've seen them try. One of the things we see often (which comes from good, albeit misinformed, intentions) is an action guided by "thinking is critically important for our kids, so let's create a sophomore year critical thinking skills course." Unfortunately, that's too late and misses the point. Students learn information in every single class period and during every day in every grade. Thinking is the thing that's going to help them structure this information and transform it into useable knowledge. Thinking isn't something they need to do only in their sophomore year.

It's something that needs to occur all the time, right alongside the content curriculum, step by step.

Another "solution" we see a lot is a bit like a Hail Mary pass. Because educators know thinking is really important but they don't know how to teach it, they assume that increasing the bandwidth will fix the problem. Just make the pipe bigger so *more* information gets to the students. Give them more AP classes, more standards, more specificity, more detail, more content, and more focus on assessment. When we chat with these educators, we get the sense that their hearts are in the right place and they're hoping for a miracle. We seem to believe that children will learn to think on their own: If we just keep teaching them more stuff, then they will magically, miraculously, somehow, someway, learn to think along the way. It reminds us of one of our favorite cartoons (Figure 4).

"I THINK YOU SHOULD BE MORE EXPLICIT HERE IN STEP TWO."

Figure 4

We go around the country in order to let teachers know that the miracle isn't happening. When you're done with your students, they go to colleges and universities, and the vast majority of them cannot think! We don't need a miracle to teach thinking and fix our schools. We need a method.

Enough with the preamble: Now we get to the meat of the book. There is a method for teaching thinking in your classroom. It won't require you to replace everything you've been doing with something new but it will allow you to do what you're already doing better and give you some ideas for some things you're not doing. It will allow you to teach thinking skills to your students, not as an add-on but as a way to get them to understand what they're required to know for the test and how they know it. In order to understand this method, first and foremost, you'll need to understand the concept of universality because we're about to learn that all knowledge is structured by four universal structures.

u·ni·ver·sal·i·ty *noun* the character or state of being universal; existence or prevalence everywhere.

It's hard to imagine that something as complex as human knowledge and cognition could be rooted in four universal structures. But it is. Indeed, one of the things that scientists have learned in the past 50 years or so is that wildly complex systems are, more often than not, based on very simple underlying rules or laws. Examples are plentiful. The evolution of the vast diversity of species and organisms on the planet are the result of simple DNA combinations and interactions. The complex patterns in a sea shell, a leopard's spots, bird flocks, schooling fish, a busy ant colony, people's movements on crowded city sidewalks, and highway traffic patterns are all are based on simple rules. Reflect on the times that you've met truly gifted scientists, CEOs, or sages who, despite their near encyclopedic knowledge and expertise, seem to have reduced their craft to a few essential principles. From social systems to natural and physical systems, the most complex among them are not complicated underneath, but simple. Thinking is no different—it is a complex adaptive system with simple underlying rules. If you're having trouble understanding what we mean by this, let's take a look at an analogy that might help you to get the gist of it. Imagine that the blob in Figure 5 contains every organism that has ever lived or is alive today or will be alive in the future. All of those organisms are the result of unique combinations of four simple molecules (ATCG) in DNA.

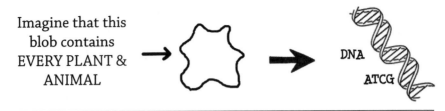

Figure 5

Now imagine that the blob in Figure 6 contains every idea that has ever been had, is being had now, or will be had in the future by any person.

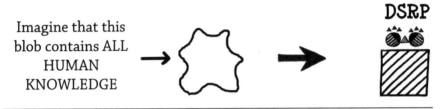

Figure 6

All of those ideas (knowledge itself) are based on four, simple, universal structures called DSRP. This book explicates four simple universal structures that underlie the process of creating knowledge: the DSRP Method.

- Distinctions: We make distinctions between things.
- Systems: We organize things into systems of parts and wholes.
- Relationships: We relate things to each other.
- Perspectives: We do all of this actions from various perspectives.

Because these structures can be thought of as a definition for thinking, we can now define the T in our equation for education:

$$\text{knowledge} = \text{information} \times \text{thinking\{DSRP\}}$$

or

$$K = I \times T\{DSRP\}$$

These four universal structures are simple, sublime, universal, and accessible. Once you understand DSRP you will find that the method can be used in your classroom at every moment with every student in every subject area or grade. In fact, as you learn more about how to teach with these simple rules in mind, you will see that their utility transcends the arena of teaching and education. DSRP will transform the way you teach and the way your students learn.

The universal structures will help you and your students develop their metacognition, or thinking about their thinking. They will provide students with a universal scaffold upon which they build all of their knowledge, access their prior knowledge, and construct new meanings for content throughout their educational experience. Of greater implication is that this holds true for every student regardless of ability, socioeconomic background, language, special needs, or age. The four simple rules apply to every grade, every lesson, every subject, and every student.

When we recognize these universal structures and explicitly use them in our teaching, it has a transformative effect on our students and ourselves. From the students' earliest days of watching *Sesame Street* to the moment when they walk across a university stage to receive their doctorates, these four simple universal structures will equip them with all they need to move up through grade levels, think through any problem, understand each subject, and prepare them for a certain future in an uncertain, fast-paced, ever-changing world. When our graduates are armed with DSRP, they will know how to do what many of today's graduates cannot: They will know how to think through anything, especially the unstructured tasks they will face in whatever vocation they choose.

Now that we've added DSRP to our equation for education, we can see that DSRP has massive implications for everything we do in education. In fact, we can take this equation as the most fundamental law of education. It should alter every aspect of your practice. Without meaningful structure (e.g., thinking), you and your kids will never get knowledge. Students will always end up being information-full.

The content that you teach (shown in Figure 7 below)—whether you're a pre-K teacher, a middle-school history teacher, an AP chemistry teacher, an art teacher, a PE or football coach, or a school counselor—is already implicitly structured with DSRP. Your students—every single one of them, regardless of age, sex, gender, culture, language, or learning style—are already using DSRP. You are already using DSRP in the classroom. So, if it's already happening, why do you need to know the method?

Because the DSRP Method will give you and your students and colleagues a language with which to communicate your thinking. It will help you to become more aware of your thinking. Awareness of one's own thinking is called metacognition. In turn, metacognition creates an

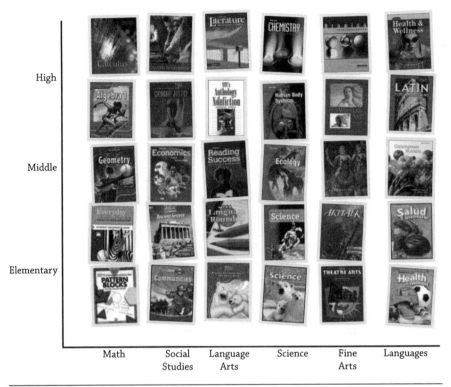

Figure 7

awareness of how one learns, which is absolutely essential to becoming a good learner. Using DSRP explicitly (you already use it implicitly) will help you to see where your thinking went wrong and how to correct it; when you have bias and how to recognize it; how disparate subjects are interconnected. It will increase your speed of knowing. Because DSRP focuses your attention on what is being constructed rather than what is being memorized, it will completely transform your practice into a learner-centered mode of teaching. It will keep the focus where it should be: on the constructions of learners. Finally, because DSRP is universal across grades and subject matter, it will increase transfer. Transfer is the most important educational outcome we can hope for, and here's why. Transfer means that you can teach a student something in one realm and he or she can apply it in a different realm. The terms "vertical transfer" and "horizontal transfer" describe how a student could learn something in one subject (English) and then apply it in another (math). That's horizontal transfer. A vertical transfer is when a student learns something in third grade that he can apply in fourth grade, or even in 10th grade or as an adult. If a student has high transfer skills, she can learn one thing and then teach herself 10, 50, or 100 additional things. In other words, if a student has high transfer, she becomes her own best teacher, which is part and parcel of becoming a lifelong learner. Using the DSRP Method in the classroom has many positive results, which we will discuss later in the book. But three outcomes should be highlighted because they form a kind of Holy Grail (or "hat trick" or "triple crown" if you will) of educational outcomes. When teachers use the DSRP Method, they see results in three important areas:

1. Increased metacognition (e.g., a student becomes his or her own best teacher/lifelong learner)
2. Increased deep understanding (e.g., the student passes school tests and life tests)
3. Increased transfer (e.g., the student makes vertical and horizontal connections)

These three outcomes are not the only outcomes of teaching with the DSRP Method, but they are the most important. There are a host of other educational outcomes, which include the following:

- Making teachers' lives easier by offering a universal formula for education that integrates many of the most popular educational frameworks (e.g., Bloom's taxonomy, understanding by design, differentiation, cooperative learning, multiple intelligences)
- National standards of thinking skills to match and support national standards of learning
- A method that makes it possible to integrate the curriculum vertically and horizontally
- A comprehensive and viable solution to the serious educational problems that we face
- Powerful tools to incorporate nonlinguistic representations (NLR) across the curriculum
- A single method for teaching all six types of 21st-century thinking skills (creativity, critical thinking, systems thinking, scientific thinking, interdisciplinary thinking, and prosocial/emotional intelligence)
- Powerful tools to inoculate young people from the onslaught of manipulative advertisements and marketing based on neuromarketing to our underlying thinking processes (thereby making better, more informed citizens)

- Various best practices, tools, and frameworks that are borne out of DSRP that transform older models like Bloom's taxonomy, planning-teaching-assessment, note taking, and so on

We'll spend more time on these outcomes at the end of the book. Let's take a final look at what our educational equation tells us in the representation in Figure 8.

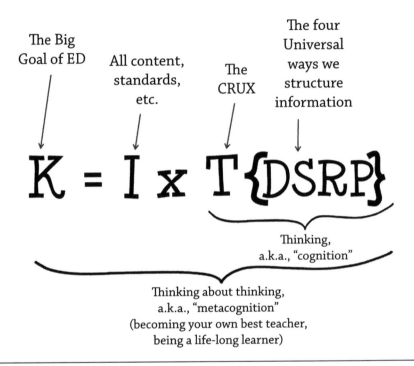

Figure 8

The power of the formula is that it tells us exactly how to create a system that creates knowledge-able students and how to avoid a system that creates information-full students. It tells us that the information (the content curriculum, standards of learning, facts, etc.) is absolutely an essential part of the equation (I). It also tells us that information is not the same thing as knowledge and that in order to get knowledge, we need to teach thinking (T) *alongside* the curriculum. Finally, the formula gives us a definition and a method for thinking, with four universal structures that we can use to teach thinking and content side by side. The formula also shows us the difference between thinking (what's called cognition by scientists) and thinking about thinking (or metacognition). Metacognition is an absolutely essential part of human learning; when learners are aware that they are in the process of learning and are aware of how they learn, learning proceeds faster and more deeply.

It bears repeating that the formula doesn't say that thinking is more important than information. Indeed, the formula says they're on equal footing. Both are required for knowledge to be formed. What the equation does say, however, is that thinking is the crux of the issues we face today. Because we have overemphasized and overengineered the curriculum (I) and because we have neglected thinking for some time now, it's clear what needs to be done to fix the problem. We need to put the T back in the equation! This is precisely why we unshackled ourselves from the halls of academe and left the ivory tower to form a movement with a simple vision: "thinking at every desk." It's a simple idea. We won't stop until every child in the United States and then the world is being explicitly taught to think.

We live in a fast-paced, globalized world where knowledge is growing and changing at a rate we can't keep up with. Our schools need to prepare students for jobs that don't exist, that will use technology not yet invented, to solve unknown problems in a society we can only imagine. In this 21st century, students need not only to know the content knowledge covered in school, they also will need to know how to think. As research scientists, educators, and entrepreneurs, we've seen the need for thinking skills all around us—from preschool to middle school, from high school to college, from business leaders to world leaders. Today's students can ace any test but lack the ability to do the unstructured tasks that are so common in the real world. Thinking is not important just in schools but also for our businesses and our country as a whole. Thinking is patriotic—it lies at the core of our workforce and can create a competitive advantage in the world.

National Standards for Thinking Skills

Now that we have the method, we also have a discrete set of things to measure. Because the DSRP Method and guiding questions offer an algorithm for sophisticated thinking, they also provide a discrete set of standards and skills that can be measured.

Standard	Skill
Learns to make distinctions by identifying what is and is not included in an idea	Names and defines concepts by communicating what something is and is not
	Considers alternative boundaries between what is and is not part of an idea
	Understands that every thing is a distinction comprised of identity and and other
Learns to think about interrelationships between and among ideas	Relates ideas
	Identifies and names hidden relationships between and among ideas
	Identifies the parts of a relationship
	Understands that every idea can be related to other ideas or can act as a relationship
Learns to think in systems by organizing parts and wholes	Identifies the parts of ideas
	Organizes systems into parts and wholes
	Recognizes the alternative wholes that a part can belong to
	Understands that every whole has parts and every part is a whole
Learns to take different points of view and see new perspectives	Takes multiple perspectives on a topic or issue
	Understands that perspective is comprised of both a point and a view
	Demonstrates taking various types of perspectives (physical, psychosocial, conceptual)
	Recognizes that a perspective exists even when it is unstated
Integrates DSRP	Demonstrates ability to combine distinction making, interrelating, part/whole organization, and perspective-taking processes to create, understand, and change concepts
Applies DSRP to content	Is aware (metacognitive) of both content and structural context when constructing the meaning of any idea ($K = I \times T\{DSRP\}$)

The standards and skills are universally important from pre-K to PhD, for every learner, at any age, at any grade, and in any subject area. The DSRP Method gives us the ability to establish national standards for thinking skills.

Implant or Inoculation?

The four structures of DSRP are universal to all thought. They are as powerful as they are ubiquitous. We often like to say that they are "hidden in plain sight." The power of these universal structures lies in seeing them all around us. We must shift our thinking to see not just the identity of something but the implied—and often purposefully ignored—other of something. Of equal importance is our ability to see the multitude of potential relationships between ideas and to recognize relationships that are implied by others on our behalf. When we organize systems, we must see the parts in the wholes and the whole in the parts. Finally, and of no less importance, is our understanding that a perspective is composed of a point and a view. If we fail to teach our students these four structures that are universal to all thinking, we allow others to use these same structures against them.

In other words, these four universal structures can be used as implants to manipulate our youth, and ourselves, for attention, money, or votes. Just as the four universal structures can be used with deleterious effect, they also serve as an inoculation against the rampant manipulation that permeates our media and society today. We can inoculate our students to offset the risk of cognitive implants by teaching them the four simple structures that are part and parcel of their thinking. We must teach students to take these steps:

- Take another look at the other.
- Discover hidden connections between ideas.
- See both the parts and wholes that make up a system.
- Take many perspectives on any and every idea they encounter.

It is essential for educators working with the DSRP Method to bring to light the hidden identities and others of our distinctions, the hidden parts and wholes of our systems, the hidden cause-and-effect relationships we draw, and the hidden points and views that make up our perspectives. These hidden structures—left unrecognized—pose the single biggest threat we have faced to this day. We run the danger of continuing to be an un-thinking society. In America, that is unacceptable. The Founding

Fathers knew they were in for a fight when they wrote the Declaration of Independence. They were thinkers, not warmongers, but they were fed up.

In the Declaration of Independence, when the term "united States of America" is used, the writers did not capitalize the word "United" as we do today. It was an adjective that described the States of America, rather than part of the proper noun it is today. But what really unites us as Americans—what creates a sense of patriotism—are the ideas expounded upon in a small paragraph in the Declaration: "We hold these truths to be self-evident, that all men are created equal, that they are endowed by their Creator with certain unalienable Rights, that among these are Life, Liberty and the pursuit of Happiness.—That to secure these rights, Governments are instituted among Men, deriving their just powers from the consent of the governed." "Deriving their just powers from the consent of the governed" is a powerful concept and it is as American as it gets. But if the governed are not thinking, then their consent is meaningless. Thinking is as patriotic and American as apple pie. We must get thinking back into the equation and at every desk.

Further Explanation of the DSRP Method

As we have just shared with you, there is a powerful equation for education. That version was a bit watered-down, as the actual equation is more complicated. We've found in our trainings that teachers like to see the more complex version and know about it. It is shown as Figure 9. You need not understand all the other parts of the equation to use the DSRP Method. All you should know is that we took a powerful scientific, mathematical theory of metacognition and translated it into an accessible classroom method that transforms teaching and learning. For educational purposes, the DSRP Method can be stated very simply. Humans use the four universal structures of distinctions, systems, relationships, and perspectives to organize knowledge of any kind. However, these structures are not used in a linear way.

$$ K = I\{\forall d\} \otimes T\left\{ : D_o^i, S_w^p, R_e^c, P_v^\rho \right\} $$

Figure 9

DSRP is the first *universal* theory of education. It has been translated to an accessible and useful method for teaching in the classroom. It leads to a deeper understanding of lesson content and develops the metacognition of both the student and teacher. The transformative effect of this method and its corresponding tools is remarkable, as it cuts across all subject areas and grade levels of students. We translated this powerful method into a number of frameworks and tools that are easy for teachers to use. We don't cover every one of the tools and frameworks in this book but we do cover the most essential ones. Any of the tools and frameworks can be used by the teacher or by the teacher and student:

1. A series of *guiding questions* for each of the four universal structures used to frame a teacher's inquiry and the student's deep understanding of the topic at hand.

2. A "root list" for each universal structure, explicated in each subsequent chapter, to help teachers understand how each structure lies at the root of many common cognitive processes and activities that are already occurring in your classroom.

3. A new, simple diagramming method called DSRP diagrams, which is similar to but more refined than mind mapping. The diagrams allow teachers to outline their full lesson plans—both the content they hope to teach and the salient thinking skills they hope to develop. This same tool is used by students to model prior knowledge and demonstrate understanding of the teacher's goal knowledge for any lesson.

4. The purposeful use of tactile manipulatives and experiential learning to reify abstract concepts in any given lesson.

5. A clear set of higher-order thinking skills that both the teacher and student will work toward in concert with a deeper understanding of lesson content.

The DSRP Method is explained in the following chapters in both theoretical and practical terms to each universal structure. Examples of work done in classrooms within various subjects and grades are also provided. This breadth of examples will show the ease with which any teacher can change his or her approach to teaching in hopes of developing both mastery of content and proficiency of thought in all students.

Knowing the results you can expect is helpful when looking for them. Infusion of the DSRP Method throughout a standards-based curriculum will have the following impact on your classroom or school:

1. Students are more engaged.

2. They understand the content more deeply.

3. Their knowledge retention increases.

4. Their transfer of learning increases.

5. They develop skills in metacognition, understanding how they think.

5. Teachers can reach any type of learner.

6. Teacher preparation is simplified.

7. A vertical articulation of essential thinking skills occurs across the grades in all subject areas.

8. Thinking skills become easy to measure with a practical way to assess how students are constructing meaning.

9. The DSRP Method develops essential skills for your students' success in the 21st century. It simplifies teaching for teachers and learning for students.

In each chapter that follows and that looks more closely at the four universal structures of the DSRP Method, we will review the root list, guiding questions, DSRP diagrams, a few vignettes that help to give each structure context, and selected case studies we have recorded over the years with teachers and students. The case examples included in each of the following four chapters show that this approach to teaching and learning can have profound effects on both teachers and students.

It's not a surprise that the hardest point to relay about this method is also the most salient benefit it brings to education as a whole. While each and every lesson you will read about is remarkable, the aggregation of them shows something far more powerful. An example is transfer—the ability to learn something in one domain (e.g., math) and use it in another domain (e.g., music). There are a few types of transfer. Near transfer occurs when a student learns something in one domain that he or she can use again in the same domain. For example, if a student learns about the states of matter and later uses that same method to characterize rocks as solids, he or she has transferred knowledge *near* the same general topic area (matter). Far transfer occurs when a student learns something in one domain and then applies it to another domain. For example, if a student learns to recognize patterns in mathematical equations, and then recognizes patterns in music, or quilt patterns—he or she has transferred that skill *far*, across many domains.

Vertical and horizontal transfer refers to educational settings where students are engaged in learning across grades and across subject areas. When a student transfers knowledge or skills across subject areas, we call it horizontal transfer. When a student transfers knowledge or skills from a lower grade to a higher grade, we call it vertical transfer.

Contrary to the teacher's experience in which a teacher stays predominantly in a single grade and subject area, a student's entire educational experience is made up of both horizontal and vertical transfers of knowledge. Therefore, for teaching and education to be student- or learner-centered it is critical to take into account this wider view as we plan, teach, and assess learning. The student-centered experience is across grades and across subject matter types. Yet, what typically occurs within grades and inside of subject matter types ignores this important fact. The DSRP Method allows students to build constructs of important ideas that can be further built upon (vertically articulated) in subsequent grades. In addition, because the DSRP Method focuses on universal structures of thinking and knowledge, it facilitates the cross-pollination of ideas from subject to subject (horizontal articulation).

Students who lack the ability to transfer and articulate their knowledge on both the horizontal and vertical axes leave their educational years without the skills needed to approach new knowledge with competence. They are more likely to be information-full than their peers. While these students may pass the tests, graduate, and go out and find employment, they are also the students who lack the independent, adaptive, problem-solving skills needed to thrive in life and to participate in and contribute to a thriving democracy. What all parents, teachers, business leaders, and politicians hope for are students who leave their educational years with a highly integrated, flexible ability with knowledge—knowledge-ability. These graduates become tomorrow's leaders, innovators, and decision makers.

What this means is that teachers who use the DSRP Method can powerfully impact not only the learning that goes on in their classrooms, but also lifelong learning. It needs no explanation that a country full of life-long learners is a country that is vital and thriving. Bar none, the best way to build lifelong learners is to help them to learn to be metacognitive and to understand how to build ideas. The best way to build a vital country or civilization is to build lifelong learners. Teachers are civilization builders when they teach their students to be knowledge builders.

We believe, and the research shows, that the biggest impacts on systems occur from the ground up and are based on the dynamics of scaling.

What this means is that the only lasting change and the only viable change will come from transforming the teacher-student relationship in the classroom. It is from the combined effects of many teacher-student interactions that our school system, our country, and our world will evolve for the better. Thinking at every desk represents this vision. We hope to create a movement to change the world, one desk, one mind, one teacher, one classroom at a time.

We hope you'll join us.

CHAPTER TWO

Distinctions

One of these things is not like the other . . .
—*Sesame Street*

To say that distinctions are all around us is a gross understatement. They are so ubiquitous that we often don't see them or forget that we are making them. Becoming more metacognitive of the distinctions we make will help us to be more creative, more analytical, and more aware of the meaning that we and our students are making.

As you will see, for each of the four universal structures—distinctions, systems, relationships, and perspectives—there are a number of simple things you can do in the classroom to help yourself and your students to be more metacognitive, to share in a common language of thinking, and to reap the rewards of being more aware of what you and your students are already doing. One point that bears repeating—and we'll continue to repeat it throughout the next four chapters—is that you and your students are already doing DSRP. DSRP is not a new pedagogical framework that you need to add to your already long and growing list of educational frameworks used in the classroom. Instead, DSRP is simply how you, your students, and the roughly seven billion other humans on Earth think. If you and your students are already thinking by using DSRP, then what's the point of the DSRP Method? The point of the DSRP Method is to give you a language to discuss and understand your thinking, to allow you to be more metacognitive about your thinking, and to encourage you to purposefully and explicitly think in certain variations of DSRP that you otherwise might not have chosen to at any given moment.

In our many trainings with teachers, we find that a few simple tools can help teachers get started in using DSRP in the classroom. First, it's important to understand what each of the four universal structures is and how it works. For this, we provide a "root list" for each of the four. The root list helps teachers immensely because it helps them realize that we're not talking about four new, never-been-used structures of thinking but four very old, always in use, universal structures. For example, here's the root list for making distinctions. As you read the list, you'll understand that you and your students are making distinctions every second of every day. You'll also see the importance of distinction making because it is the root of everything on this list:

> compare, contrast, define, differentiate, name, label, is, is not, identity, recognize, identify, exist, other, boundary, select, equals, does not equal, similar, different, same, opposite, us/them, thing, notthing, something, element; the prefix a- (as in a-gnostic); recognize, single out, pick out, pinpoint, put a name to, know, discern, remember, determine, establish, ascertain, make out, diagnose, discern, verify, confirm, bracket, put side by side with, juxtapose, liken to, equate to, variation, contradiction, incongruity, opposition, polarity, similarity, synonym, antonym, antithesis, foil, complement, disagree, agree, resemble, object, article, item, artifact, commodity, device, gadget, instrument, utensil, tool, implement, entity, body, whatsit, whatchamacallit, identification, ID, title, tag, label, dub, specify, choose, select, pick, decide on, nominate, designate, describe, mark, stamp, pigeonhole, stereotype, typecast, exist, be alive, occur, happen, take place, come about, arise, crop up, transpire, materialize, ensue

At least once per nanosecond, you do one of these things. You simply can't go through life without recognizing something. In order to walk without tripping, you have to distinguish between your body and physical objects in your path. So, you and your students are making a nearly infinite number of distinctions every day. Not all of them need to be discussed, of course, but a few of them need to be highlighted as relevant, important, interesting, and of note.

In fact, every concept or word that a child comes to understand throughout his or her entire life is a distinction that is constantly being re-informed and adjusted as new knowledge comes to light. Here's a simple example, but you can imagine that the same is true for any object or idea (an apple, a dog, the universe, an atom). In the National Science Education Standards (1996 NAP, http://www.nap.edu/openbook.php?record_id=4962&page=21) the standard for science literacy is as follows: Students should develop an understanding of what science is, what science is not, what science can and cannot do, and how science contributes to culture. Note that even at a young age we begin working on the distinction "science"—what it is and what it is not. Both what it is and what it is not are equally important in understanding science. Likewise, this identity other (is/is not) interaction is necessary to understand any thing or idea. Over time, students develop an ability to distinguish between science and not science but the distinction continues to expand with increased sophistication over their life spans. Still, today, scientists are debating what is and is not science. Artists are debating what is and is not art. Legislators are debating what is and is not torture. Politicians are debating what is and is not good for the country. Pick any word in the English language out of thin air and explore it as a distinction. How do you know what that word means and does not mean? How did you come to know that? That is the process of distinction making. We are constantly doing it and will continue to do so.

Speaking of words, when you think about the vocabulary list you might associate with any lesson, that's a simple way of understanding the distinctions that are important. So, in 10th-grade chemistry, some of the important distinctions that need to be understood are bromine, chlorine, mercury, uranium, and zirconium. To understand any single chemical element, it's actually very helpful to understand other elements. Distinction making provides a simple truth: To understand what gives something a unique identity, we must understand the things that it is not. In particular, we come to understand a thing's uniqueness by exploring those other things that are closest to it. Sure, a child can better understand an apple by understanding it's not a toaster, but a hard pear is a much better shill.

Another invaluable resource for teachers in our trainings is the set of guiding questions for each universal structure. These are simple "Mad Lib" style questions that can be used universally for any topic or grade. The exact wording of the questions is not important—there are many ways the same question could be worded differently. Also, the questions guide teachers to think about how to ask questions. Sometimes this means that the questions are asked of the students themselves, but in other cases it just means that the teacher uses the questions to guide his or her own thinking or to help to better understand the student's thinking. The ways that a teacher can use the questions are varied but there are only a small number of questions necessary, which makes the teacher's life easier. Think of the DSRP guiding questions as a new form of Socratic questioning for the 21st century. Where the Socratic method of questioning leads students to a black-and-white view of the world, DSRP questions lead students to see the infinite shades of gray that actually exist in the world. This is called multivalent or many-faceted logic, whereas Socratic inquiry (the basis for our traditional educational inquiry paradigm) leads us to believe that the world is bivalent or two-faceted. When you begin to see how D works with S, R, and P, you'll see a powerful new logic emerge. The DSRP guiding questions for D are:

What can you tell me about _____?

What is _____?

What is not _____?

There are lots of different ways to ask or think about such questions, and not all of them involve literally asking a question. For example, if you ask your students "What is a scientist?" you might get answers (depending on the grade) such as an academic, a person who studies a topic, has a lab, investigates using the scientific method, knows stuff, a geek, wears a white lab coat, and so on. Then, if you ask your students "What is not a scientist?" you might get answers like a dog, an apple, or a car is not a scientist, or alternatively the negation of the answers they gave you for what is a scientist such as not an academic, doesn't study a topic, doesn't have a lab, and so forth.

These distinction-type activities and questions for lower grades are very useful. But distinction making is really about distinguishing between things that are near-neighbors, things that are almost the same but not the same. For example, distinguish between an equation and an expression in mathematics. Or, distinguish between an apple and a crab apple. Between a tree and a bush. Distinguish between a car and a racecar. Distinguish between a war and a conflict. Between a terrorist and a revolutionary. Between sympathy and empathy. Take any of these examples of near-neighbor distinctions and you will see that they have the same structure of identity/other. The difference is in the sophistication, the granularity of the distinctions being made. So, while a first grader might distinguish between a scientist and a not scientist by constructing that a scientist is a person and a not scientist is a dog, as their distinctions get more sophisticated they will use the same identity/other structure to differentiate between a scientist and an engineer or a scientist and an academic, or between a scientist and an auto mechanic who is hypothesis testing a nonfunctioning radiator. The key to asking distinction-making questions is two-fold. First, recognize the identity/other structure of all distinctions. Second, guide your students increasingly toward distinctions between things that are near-neighbors, that is, things that are nearly, but not entirely, synonymous.

DSRP diagrams are powerful tools used by teachers and students for nonlinguistic representations (NLRs) of content curriculum. Best practices show that while using graphic organizers is a good practice, many graphic organizers will trap students in thinking cul-de-sacs, or biased thinking. In contrast, DSRP diagrams are a universal graphic organizer that ensures that students will construct knowledge in ways that are based on the existing structures of knowledge. In other words, many existing graphic organizers provide an arbitrary structure for a student's thinking for them (e.g., a fish bone, a radial centralized map, etc.), whereas DSRP Diagrams place the onus on a student to think deeply about the content and structure of their thoughts using distinctions, systems, relationship and perspectives.

The beauty of the DSRP diagrams is that with a very small palette of simple images, a teacher or student can diagram anything from the simplest idea to the most sophisticated ideas known to mankind. The entire palette for DSRP diagrams is shown in Figure 10. When we draw distinctions, we are representing two important ideas. First, any idea or object that we draw is an identity. We can use squares, circles, or triangles to represent an identity. So, for example, if we want to begin thinking about different types of fruits we can draw them as shown in Figure 11.

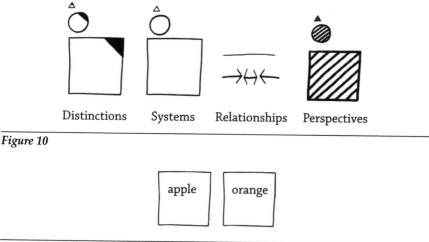

Distinctions   Systems   Relationships   Perspectives

Figure 10

apple   orange

Figure 11

We can see that apples are distinctly different from oranges (visually speaking) because they are not in the same shape. The two squares are different, which represents that the two ideas or objects are different. However, we also want to get across that there is a deep relationship between the two distinct entities. Namely, to understand one, you must understand the other and vice versa. That is, not only is an apple an apple (what it is) but it's also not an orange (what it isn't). We can write this in this way by giving both items their two respective labels (see Figure 12). But now let's add some complexity. There are more than two types of fruits. Let's add some fruits (see Figure 13). Notice that when we do, we see six more identities. But also notice that we have all the not-identities as well.

apple
not-orange

orange
not-apple

Figure 12

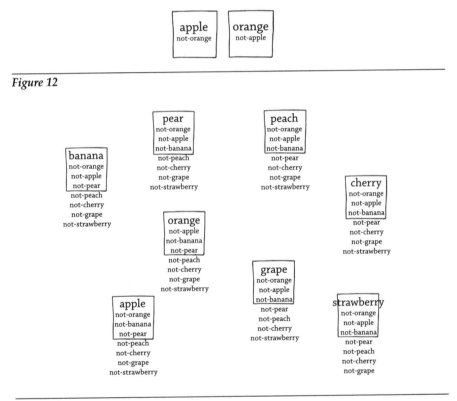

Figure 13

As you can see, this adds a lot of extra stuff to the graphic representation and can lead to clutter. We know that all identities are being co-defined not only by what they are (the identity) but also by what they are not (other), but do we really need this much stuff cluttering up our diagram? No. But we do need to represent that underlying structure in some way when it's important to highlight. So, we can draw in little black corners to represent the "otherness" of all the "not apples" (see Figure 14). Think about what this image is saying to check if it makes sense. Think about the process by which a small child comes to know about an apple: not only by touching, seeing, and tasting an apple but also by having the same experiences with not-apples (e.g., bananas, pears, oranges). When a child tastes an apple, her distinction of what an apple is increases in sophistication from merely seeing one but when she then tastes a banana, she not only increases her understanding of bananas but of apples as well. So, although this diagram is visually simple, it represents a number of complex ideas. Namely, it shows that the distinctions being shown are between each identity and its set of others. That's a lot of cognitive complexity being represented in a very simple way!

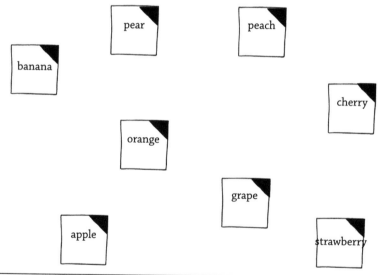

Figure 14

But what if we don't want to represent all that complexity? Sometimes it's unimportant that every identity is interacting with its set of others. Instead, we want to zero in on and highlight one particular distinction—to draw attention to it. For example, let's say we want to distinguish between equations and expressions (something that is difficult for many students). In Figure 15, we use the black marks to highlight the salient distinction that's being made. Notice that while each of the objects is an identity (part of a distinction), not all of the objects have a black mark. Only two of the objects do, because that is the point of this lesson—to distinguish between equations and expressions. So, while really every object in the diagram is an identity/other distinction that interacts with every other object in the diagram, we've used the distinction marker to highlight the most salient distinction and the focus of the standard of learning. What students see is that equations and expressions are exactly the same except equations contain an equal sign. You'll learn more about how the circles and triangles are used later in Chapter 3.

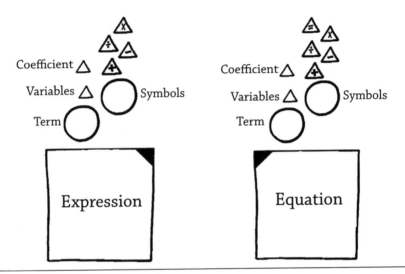

Figure 15

The distinctions we make, recognize, or more importantly don't recognize, have wide-reaching implications in our personal and professional lives in arenas ranging from science to geopolitics. To see the deep importance that distinction making plays in our lives, we will take you on a journey through several vignettes. Each one is interesting in its own right, but taken together, you will see how pervasive and important distinctions are. You may also be surprised to see how invisible they are and how often your behavior is based on things that are not in your conscious awareness. Let's get started. From the mountains of Italy to the innards of our own families, from prelinguistic babies to Pentagon consultants, from geopolitical maps to manipulative motives, from the superficial to the salient and from preschool to a PhD, and in both simple and sublime ways, distinction making is a purposeful and powerful aspect of human cognition. Indeed, it is universal to every thought we have ever had, are having right now, or will have for the rest of our days.

Distinctions: Identity/Other

Any time we make a distinction, we assign each idea an identity and create, in so doing, an invisible other. When we say "us," for example, we establish "us" as an identity. But we also, inadvertently, often unconsciously, imply an invisible other: "them." No matter what we are thinking, we are making distinctions and those distinctions follow this universal structure: distinctions = identity + other (see Figure 16). It makes no difference whether the idea is dog, the Revolutionary War, John's wardrobe, the Treaty of Versailles, Manifest Destiny, Congress, the town of Ithaca, whatever. Every distinction has the same form and the same rules are followed in order to make it.

Distinctions

identity 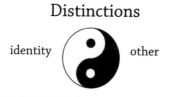 other

Figure 16

When we differentiate ideas, objects, or people, or we give concepts specific names to discern them from other concepts, we make distinctions. As we construct an idea of what something is, we also construct, either implicitly or explicitly, what something is not. Creating a distinction draws a boundary between what something is and what it is not. Indeed, we may often learn a lot about what something is not long before we know what it is. In science it is much easier to determine what is not the cause of something than what is. In the lifelong process of learning who you are, you will likely work a lot of jobs or be in several relationships that are clearly "not you," and in the process you will learn more and more about your own identity.

Distinction making is required for the most mundane activity imaginable, as well as for higher-order thinking. There is no pursuit or development of any field of knowledge without distinction making. There is no lecture, activity, or conversation in any subject matter without distinction making. Being more aware of the distinctions you are making (and their underlying structure) will make you more analytically sophisticated, more creative, more systemic in your thinking, and even more emotionally intelligent. Seeing the other when those around you do not will help you to recognize opportunities and pitfalls that others cannot see. Understanding the underlying structure of distinctions will actually make you appear to be smarter.

As we explore a few vignettes about distinction making, look for this identity/other structure. As your mind becomes more aware of this universal thinking pattern, you will start to see it everywhere and in everything you do. You will start to see how distinctions are made to explain, understand, communicate, and even to manipulate, and you will begin to feel like there's a lot you've been missing.

Naming Things

Because we use language to communicate our ideas, distinction making often means naming things. The way we name things—whether proper names for people, names of files and folders on our computer desktops, or scientific names for species—has a big impact on how we see the world. Finding the right names for things is important. It gives them identities and differentiates them from other things. When the names we give things are vague or too similar, it can lead to confusion, misunderstanding, and even chaos.

One example of confusion has come from the heavyweight boxing champ George Foreman, who has named all five of his sons George. He claimed that this made it easy to remember their names. Over time, it was hard to distinguish among them. George Sr. and his wife ended up giving each George Jr. a number from one to five (literally, George I, George II, etc.). Thus, the name George alone did not allow for a practical distinction among the five junior Georges.

As we develop conceptual models, we often either differentiate too little or not enough. Both are pitfalls of distinction making. When we make distinctions, we often think that we need to name them. And although naming can be a good indicator of a distinction, a name is not required. Young children show us that we don't need words to make distinctions. Well before he could speak, Derek's son Carter made clear distinctions on a daily basis. This was obvious at mealtime. We'd give him blueberries, strawberries, and Cheerios, and he'd line them up and eat his favorite first. Blueberries, then he'd proceed to strawberries, and then Cheerios. Carter didn't know the words for any of them, but he clearly distinguished among them. Distinction making is a universal cognitive skill that precedes language. While we use language to express the distinctions we make, we don't need language to actually make them.

George Foreman's and Carter's distinction making may seem silly in the grand scheme of things, but make no mistake, the distinctions we make are often serious. In 2004, Thomas Barnett published the Pentagon's New Map.* The map was a cornerstone of how world leaders conceptualized U.S. foreign policy in relation to terrorism between 2004 and 2009. The leading economic powers of the world ("Us") are called "the functioning core." The other countries of the world ("Them") are, by implication, part of a not-functional core, or a dysfunctional periphery. (The map labels it "the non-integrated gap.")** In this case, the functional core is the identity.

It turns out that the countries that made up the "not-functioning core" in the 2004 Pentagon map had already organized themselves under the name the Non-Aligned Movement (NAM) back in 1955. NAM has since become an international organization of 118 states that considered themselves not formally aligned with or against the two major power blocs: the United States and Western Europe versus the Soviet Republic and Eastern Europe. Most member nations had suffered the imperialism of at least one of these at some point in their history. NAM strove from its inception to provide a group identity for its member nations through nonalliance (with the others) and to strengthen themselves through alliance with one another. NAM's 118 states all come together to differentiate themselves through nonalignment.***

Alienating or ignoring the other can be detrimental. As Sun Tzu said in *The Art of War*, "If you know your enemies and know yourself, you can win a thousand battles without a single loss. If you only know yourself, but not your opponent, you may win or may lose. If you know neither yourself nor your enemy, you will always endanger yourself." Whether you choose to recognize the invisible other in order to empathize with him or to defeat him, the maxim remains the same: As a 21st-century thinker, you must see both the identity and the other in every distinction you make.

---

*Barnett, Thomas P. M. (2004). *The Pentagon's new map: War and peace in the twenty-first century.* New York: G. P. Putnam's Sons.

**http://www.thomaspmbarnett.com/pnm/map_index.htm (accessed September 30, 2008).

***This number comes from a letter from the chairman of the Coordinating Bureau of the Non-Aligned Movement, written in September 2008. It can be seen at http://domino.un.org/unispal.nsf/47d4e277b48d9d36852 56ddc00612265/38ecc57a3c2e3a7b852574da00718e !OpenDocument (accessed January 9, 2009).

Getting Our Identities From Relationships With the Other

There's a tribe in Northern Natal in South Africa that uses the greeting "Sawubona"; this literally translates as "I see you." Once seen, the person being greeted responds, "Sikhona," or "I am here." The exchange is borne of the spirit of *ubuntu*, a word that stems from the folk saying "A person is a person because of other people."

In other words, our identity is based on recognition by another that we exist. We are all defined by how we relate to others in context. At home, we are "parents" and "spouses" to those around us; at work we are "CEOs" or "assistants." This is in contrast to our typical notion that our identities come from within; in fact, we get our identities from those around us (others). Identity and other are two sides of a single coin. There is no identity without an other.

Lost Identity

No man is an island, entire of itself.
  —John Donne

In September 2006, a man woke up on a street in Denver, Colorado, with no idea of who he was, where he was, or how he'd gotten there. Having no name, no identity, he was checked into a hospital as "Alpha 74."* There, medical personnel found no head injury or tumor to explain his amnesia. Officials administered truth serum to make sure he wasn't feigning his forgetfulness. In the end, he proved to be such a good, honest guy, they started calling him Al (it wasn't his name, but a more human version of "Alpha 74").

"I want my past," Al kept saying. He even made an appeal on national television to anyone who might know his identity. He needed an other in relation to whom he could find his identity and be himself. His past, if he could find it, would tell the story of who he was and provide those others who ultimately defined him. Without all of that, he had no identity. The TV appearances worked. Al was identified as Jeffrey Ingram, and he returned to his home in Olympia, Washington. Once he found others, he also found his identity.

---

*Komo 4 News and ABC News. (2006, October 22). Missing Olympia man found in Denver. http://www.komonews.com/news/4454227.html (accessed November 7, 2008).

You Are Entering Not-Cadola

It's common in the United States to be greeted with a sign that reads "Entering Smallville" when driving into a town by that name and to see

a sign saying "Leaving Smallville" when driving out. These signs demarcate the distinct area, the boundaries, of Smallville. This is in contrast to towns in other countries, for example, Cadola, Italy. We encounter the same type of sign upon entrance, but as we drive out at the other side of town, the same sign shows up again—but crossed through with a red line. As we leave Cadola, we enter not-Cadola.

Figure 17

Distinction Making in Seconds or Years

The making of distinctions is so pervasive, so ever-present, that it is hard to recognize all of the distinctions that happen around us all of the time. In less than a second, we can make dozens or more distinctions. Then, in another split second, those distinctions morph into new ones. Distinctions occur in fractions of a second within our own minds, but they also occur over weeks, months, years, decades, even centuries, as social groups and whole cultures struggle to define things. Let's look at three different distinctions—two that happen fast in your mind and one that occurred slowly, over many years, and among many minds.

The way you interpret a Rubin vase (created by the Gestalt psychologist Edgar Rubin) depends on how you define the borders of the drawing. Look at the white area of the image in Figure 18. Do you see a vase? Now look at the black area. Do you see two faces? With a little concentration, most people will see both faces and a vase. But is that all you see? No matter how many times you ask, people tend only to see the identities: the faces and the vase. But what you are actually seeing are four variables: face and not-face

Figure 18

and vase and not-vase. Notice, too, that we can't see both at the same time. When we're looking at the faces, the vase no longer exists as a vase but becomes simply a not-face. Likewise, when we focus on the vase, the faces become the other, or not-vase. As you can see, an awareness of identity/other allows us to see more possibilities; therefore, the depth of our understanding expands.

What we choose to see or are able to recognize changes everything: how we think, how we behave, and how we understand the world.* Any time we make a distinction, we decide to recognize some things and to ignore others. We make one thing primary and another secondary. Let's try another example.

What do you see in Figure 19? An old woman or a young lady? Both are in the picture. Again, it's all in how we draw the boundaries. If you see the young lady, take another look at the necklace she is wearing. It should turn into the mouth of the old woman. The Rubin vase and the image in Figure 19 are distinctions that occur within seconds. Yet, even in this tiny time span, we can see that our thinking includes elements that are part of our consciousness and other

Figure 19

elements that lie beneath our awareness. The first pattern of thinking—distinction making—will help you to see more of the processes that you or your students are using to build constructions of the world or to conclude things about it.

Now let's look at a distinction whose boundaries were interpreted and drawn not in seconds by one mind, but by thousands of highly trained minds over the course of years and years. There's been a sort of galactic patriotism in knowing there are nine planets in our solar system, and they are, in order of increasing distance from the sun, Mercury, Venus, Earth, Mars, Jupiter, Saturn, Uranus, Neptune, and Pluto. In the English-speaking world, we've had a mnemonic device to remember the order and we've taught it zealously to our children and students: My Very

---

*Many interesting examples exist of images that play with the concept of figure-ground or simply allow the viewer to play with perception by seeing things in different ways. Mooney faces, developed in the 1950s by the cognitive psychologist Craig Mooney, have a certain strange beauty. These barely sketched-in black-and-white faces work on the principle of perceptual closure, a right-brain function by which we "fill in" missing information, sometimes with very little to rely on, to conceptualize a complete image. Studies have shown that when the faces are presented upside down or in other variant orientations, they become more difficult to grasp as whole images.

Educated Mother Just Served Us Nine Pizzas. Never mind all that; even the most sacred knowledge can change. Now, perhaps our mothers can simply serve us Nothing, because Pluto was recently stripped of its planetary status.

Pluto made headlines when scientists decided it was not actually a planet.* While we all learned of this classification from planet to not-planet in an instant, in fact, changing the distinction took years. It was determined through an official vote at the General Assembly of the International Astronomical Union (IAU) in Prague in 2006. Prior to the vote, of course, a whole process took place. Individuals and teams conducted research; research findings were shared through refereed journals and conversations; people engaged in impassioned debates, and some spoke before the group at the IAU conference. One person alone can create a new distinction in seconds (as we saw with the face/vase and old/young woman figures), but a group takes much longer to gather the evidence and come to an agreement. Yet, the elemental structure and process remain the same: A distinction is made up of an identity and an other.

In 2003 a celestial body was first identified that was situated beyond Pluto in the solar system.** (Knowledge changes by growing.) Nicknamed "Xena," this object was determined to be larger than Pluto and, like Pluto, to have its own moon.*** This put the scientific community in a quandary, forcing a redefinition of the concept of a planet.**** As knowledge changes, distinctions once made must be revisited and revised. That's how Pluto became a dwarf planet.

Clear Boundaries Are Often Fuzzy

We often imagine that boundaries are more solid and clear-cut than they truly are. For example, the border between Italy and Austria is well defined on a map, but in reality, there is no solid line painted across the landscape. The distinctions are actually cultural and historical, and they don't clearly fall on either side of a solid line.

---

*For Derek's detailed and entertaining presentation of the entire history of Pluto, go to http://www.thinkandthrive.com/tw/files/media/Pluto.pdf (accessed October 16, 2008).

**The Adler Planetarium Statement About Pluto Reclassification. (2006, August 24). 26th General Assembly of the International Astronomical Union, p. 48. It was Michael Brown of MIT who made this discovery.

***Chang, K. (2006, April 12). Planet discovered last year, thought to be larger than Pluto, proves roughly the same size." http://www.nytimes.com/2006/04/12/science/space/12planet.html?_r=1. Chang also tells us that Xena had to be viewed through the Hubble telescope so that it could be identified. It was found to measure 2,400 kilometers across, making it 5% larger than Pluto and 30% wider.

****Adler Planetarium Statement (2006), p. 49.

If you travel the Alps from Italy to Austria, your trek will take you through the land of the Ladins.* The Ladin people, who share this region with others who identify more distinctly as Italian, speak their own language, also called Ladin. It's neither Italian nor Austrian German; it's similar to both and unlike either. In Ladin, you'll find that dumplings and sauerkraut show up on your plate well before you hit the Austrian border. You might feast on pasta and strudel in the same meal. But before you walk into the restaurant, be sure to notice how the architecture blends Italian and Austrian components. The history of this region is a story of shifting distinctions and redefinitions, as the land passed back and forth between Austria and Italy. It even belonged to Tyrol at one point. Anyone remember Tyrol?

The concept of fuzzy boundaries doesn't stop at the geographic or geopolitical level. When you zoom in wherever borders and boundaries exist, even in the conceptual realm, things blur. All distinctions start to get fuzzier, even between or among ideas. This is why such heated debate occurs when experts split hairs—because at that resolution nearly every clear-cut boundary gets fuzzy.

Fuzzy boundaries are everywhere. Even as you sit and read this, there is a distinction between you and your chair—which isn't as clear as you might think. On a molecular level, there is no line drawn between you and the chair: You're a clump of molecules, the chair is a clump of molecules, and molecules are not static. The molecules of the chair form a solid surface and interact with one another more strongly than they interact with your molecules. (This gives the chair its "chairness" and you your "you-ness." It also gives you a place to sit.) Still, a little of the force that binds objects together leaks out, and your molecules spend some time mingling with those of the chair. Thus, on a micro level, you're part of the chair when you sit on it, and the chair is part of you.** The boundary is fuzzy.

Because Boundaries Are Fuzzy, They Can Be Manipulated

Between 1810 and 1812, the quaintly named Elbridge Gerry served as the governor of Massachusetts. That was plenty of time for his party to produce an electoral map carefully planned to maximize the number of seats

---

*To view Derek's online slide show online that guides you through this trek, go to http://www.thinkan-dthrive.com/kb/questions/15/What+are+Distinctions+%28D%29%3F (accessed October 16, 2008). On that page, find the section entitled "Walking a Fuzzy Distinction" and follow the link to the slide show.

**Small interactions among different clumps of matter are called Van der Waals interactions. This is not Dutch for small but comes from the name of the Dutch scientist Johannes Diderik van der Waals. To learn more about this phenomenon, go to http://en.wikipedia.org/wiki/Van_der_Waals_force (accessed November 7, 2008).

it could win. One district was thought to be shaped like a salamander and was famously depicted by a cartoonist of the time (see Figure 20). Thus, the word "gerrymander" was born.*

Figure 20

In modern usage, gerrymandering refers to aggressive redistricting in which one party reapportions voting districts so as to increase the number of seats it will hold in the legislature. Because this is done by the party in power, gerrymandering favors incumbents.

"Put in simple English," wrote P. Harris in the British independent newspaper *The Guardian*, "gerrymandering enables politicians to choose their electors. Not the other way around."** Harris also (with some relish, and also with accuracy) described a map showing American voting districts: "They are far from logical or square. Instead they are wild shapes, huge ink blotches spraying in every direction like some weird Rorschach Test. They are also a fundamental threat to American democracy."

It's important to teach students that the boundaries we draw to make distinctions are not superfluous; they have great purpose, meaning, and impact. When we teach our students about distinction making, we inoculate them from an onslaught of manipulative messages (from media and political sources) that are vying for their time, attention, votes, and dollars. When we are made aware of the structure of our own thought, we are much less susceptible to manipulation whereas when our thoughts are hidden from our view and we are easily swayed. Hitler said, "What luck for rulers that the people do not think." He was right. Distinction making, like each of the four universal structures, can be an implant or an inoculation. It is why thinking in general is patriotic and an essential component of any democracy.

*Cox, G. W., & Katz, J. N. (2002). *Elbridge Gerry's salamander: The electoral consequences of the reapportionment revolution.* Cambridge, UK: Cambridge University Press.

**Harris, P. (2006, September 28). Gerrymandering: How U.S. politicians draw the electoral lines" [electronic version]. *Guardian Unlimited* (retrieved February 9, 2007, from http://wf2dnvr4.webfeat. org/). http:// en.wikipedia.org/wiki/Bioinformatics (accessed January 24, 2009).

Figuring Out What Something Is by What It Is Not

The children's book *The Bus for Us** shows a brother and sister standing at the bus stop on a school day. A classic yellow taxi rolls in. "Is this the bus for us, Gus?" asks the little sister. The big brother answers, "No, Tess. This is a taxi." A big blue vehicle with pulleys and cables comes along next. "Is this the bus for us, Gus?" asks Tess, only to be told it's a tow truck. This exchange continues with a fire engine, an ice-cream truck, a garbage truck, and a backhoe, until finally the big yellow school bus shows up and Gus gets to say, "Yes, Tess. This is the bus for us. Let's go." So Tess learns what a bus is by finding out what it is not. (Notice that Tess learns what a fire truck is by looking at near-neighbors with her brother, not simply by randomly thinking of things that are not a fire truck (e.g., duck, paper, star).

Of course, that's not the only distinction being made here. There's also that of us. A bus could come by that's the bus for not-us, or for them, and Gus and Tess would need to make that distinction and stay put instead of climbing aboard. This notion of understanding what something is by understanding what it is not is illustrated in classrooms every day.

Case Examples

Family

The best benefit of our work presents itself whenever we are invited into classrooms to see teachers engaging their students by using the DSRP Method. We visited one of our favorite teachers, Ms. Cunningham, in Virginia. She taught a pre-K special needs class of 14 students whose ages and developmental abilities varied. She explained her belief that her students were as capable of learning as everyone else, despite the misconception that they first needed to learn to tie their shoes before delving into the state curriculum. She started with distinction making—supported by the concept of parts and wholes. To ease the kids into these new ideas, she decided to relate distinctions to something they all knew well: their families.

Ms. Cunningham has a remarkable understanding of her students' capacity and how to reach all of them, despite the variation in their abilities. She used three different sizes of hollow blocks to give the students a way to touch the abstract ideas and keep their attention for the whole

---

*Bloom, S. (2001). *A bus for us*. Honesdale, PA: Boyds Mills Press.

lesson. She wrote the word "family" on the large block, and then placed a picture of each child on the middle-sized block. She began the lesson by showing a block with her own picture on it, which she pointed at the large block family as she said, "The parts of *my* family are myself [dropped a small block inside the middle block], my husband [dropped another small block inside the middle block], and my baby, Charlie [dropped another small block inside the middle block]." Then she turned to each student, one at a time, and had them point their picture block at the word "family." As they listed the parts of their family, they, too, dropped little blocks into the middle block to represent each member of the family. All of her students engaged in this lesson with great proficiency, engagement, and enthusiasm.

Two students stood out in their responses that are worth noting. The first, Adam, was born with Down's Syndrome. He is an open, loving, and engaged 6-year-old boy. He sat through the lesson and watched his peers list all of their family members, using the littlest blocks to represent people with great patience. He was last in the group. As Ms. Cunningham said, "Adam, who is in your family?" He carefully named a person, and plunked them into the middle-sized block. Along the way, Ms. Cunningham reinforced his pronunciation of certain sounds he is working on with his speech pathologist. Interestingly, he listed all of his family members: "Mom, Dad, John, Julie . . ." But he forgot himself. Ms. Cunningham slowed him down, asking, "Who else is in your family?" Adam looked confused, so Ms. Cunningham dumped the little blocks he had already named back out on the floor, asking Adam to point to each block and name each one. He did this with great skill. After he named the four, Ms. Cunningham dropped a fifth little block on the floor—and said, "And . . . ??" A great moment of recognition, a smile, and then he said proudly, "Adam!!" At that moment he understood his construct of family, the parts of the family, and recognized that he himself was an important part of that distinction, "Adam's family."

Another student, Jimmy, carefully listed out his mother, grandmother, father, sister . . . and then all seven of his cats as parts of his family. Ms. Cunningham aptly stopped him and helped him understand that his family had an additional distinction: pets. While this may not seem remarkable to you at first, it is. The way that Ms. Cunningham handled it both allowed Jimmy's construct of family—although different—to be heard and validated, while it also reinforced the idea of "family" that might be on a test someday. In sum, when DSRP is used to frame and implement a lesson it gets us away from the "right and wrong" paradigm and subsequently removes students' anxiety that they'll give the wrong answer and be less engaged. Because DSRP elucidates a child's construct before relaying the teacher's construct, it frees students from the fear of being wrong and demonstrates the validity of their own prior knowledge. It also gives a teacher insight into the gaps in each child's baseline construct relative to any lesson, so she knows how to better guide or course-correct throughout the lesson for each learner. Therefore, Jimmy's inclusion of his pets was not dismissed as wrong—which could create anxiety to engage generally. At the same time, it keyed Ms. Cunningham in to note that his construction needed "fine-tuning" before any state-based test was given because the test answer only includes people in the construct family.

Scientists

Ms. Green, a first-grade teacher, led to her students' deeper understanding of how we know what something is by posing the simple question, "What is a scientist?" As the students began their discussion, two things became clear. First, what a scientist is varies by each student's perspective: One student argued that a scientist is a teacher, and another agreed that scientists work in laboratories. Second, as they continued to deliberate, the students made two pieces of flip chart paper—one labeled "What is a scientist?" and the other labeled "What is NOT a scientist?" Both sheets were posted on the wall, and the students were divided into two groups in which they wrote down all characteristics they could think of onto Post-its for each sheet. In other words, we often build our understanding of what something is by understanding what something is *not*.

The students attached each Post-it to the correct sheet and the teacher was then able to review and discuss the students' collective lists to guide them into a shared construct, or understanding, of what a scientist is. While this lesson was short and simple, it was foundational to a much longer unit that introduces first graders to science, scientists, and scientific thinking more generally. By having the students come to a robust and shared understanding of this first building block for the unit, they left with a much deeper understanding of a scientist than if they had simply memorized a list of characteristics. Also, they learned the process of making a distinction. More important, because Ms. Green was explicit about the thinking skill they were developing as she delivered the lesson content, she began the critical process of developing her students' metacognitive skills. This skill will serve them throughout their educational experiences.

Torture

Ms. Darling, an AP Human Geography teacher in high school, began a month-long unit with an exercise to help her students build a definition of "torture." Using the DSRP Method she asked, "What is and isn't torture?" This was an issue of great debate in the public discourse at the time. "What information have you previously discussed or understood about torture?" Responses included "it involves physical pain," "it also includes mental suffering," and so on. As the students narrowed in to a shared understanding of the idea of torture, Ms. Darling raised the question, "Okay, so how do we know if torture should be legal or *not* legal?"— a new distinction that needed to be made to better understand the critical distinction debated in the news of what is and is not torture.

She took the opportunity to lead her students to see that the identity and other of any idea are critical to understand how we, as a society, make social constructions. Other examples included gay rights ("What is and is *not* a right?") and abortion ("What is and is *not* life?" or "What is and is *not* murder?"). As the lesson progressed, Ms. Darling showed them that how we distinguish ideas like torture, rights, legality, life, and others is the foundation to our social construction on the many issues we see in current events every day. This discussion, guided by DSRP, "focused the discussion for higher level students, and increased participation by usually less engaged students." She saw "more hands, more students eager to speak than ever before, with seven kids raising their hands at one time . . . all of them wanted to be heard!" When asked to reflect on why this was the case, Ms. Darling said, "When you frame a lesson around its content and encourage students throughout to think about their thinking, the buy-in is greater, the engagement is increased, and, ultimately, the understanding of the lesson and themselves as learners is deeper."

Many More Examples of Making Distinctions

From discussing a family and a scientist to debating about torture, rights, and life, making distinctions are part of everything we teach. Distinctions are in every thought that we have. Distinction making is essential to our clarity of concepts, setting boundaries, seeing parts and wholes as distinctions, and thinking scientifically. Distinctions are all around us: They are prelinguistic and are foundational to our ability to model what we see and understand in the universe. There are many opportunities to develop this skill in students with very little effort in existing curricula. Several examples are discussed here.

A pre-K special education teacher teaches a lesson on the standard of learning "What is a family?" by using tactile manipulatives with students (see Figure 21). Each student can bring a manipulative up and place it inside the distinction (a block or bucket) family or not-family. Students are active, engaged, and building a mental model using distinctions (and part/whole systems).

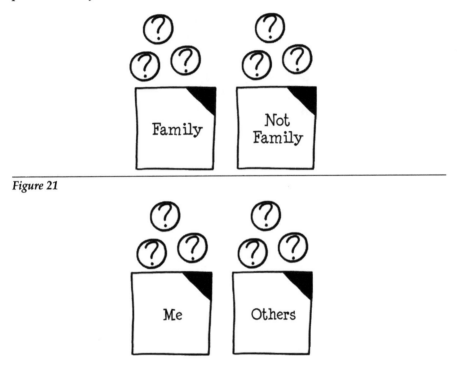

Figure 21

Figure 22

Figure 22 shows how students begin their kindergarten year with a lesson on the standard of learning called "About Me" in order to introduce themselves to one another. The students engage in drawing diagrams distinguishing qualities that are unique to themselves. The teacher then has students draw a picture detailing the items they came up with in their diagrams. Their pictures are more sophisticated than in non-DSRP classrooms because the students use their explicit mental models as guides to draw their pictures. The distinctions they make are more refined than non-DSRP classrooms. Their familiarity with the common structures and subelements (distinctions and systems and identity/other, part/whole) will pay off in the speed with which they engage and understand the material. Even though the material is new to them, the common structures are well understood.

As Figure 23 demonstrates, a first-grade teacher teaches a lesson on the standard of learning "Who are community helpers?" Although the content is different, the students have seen this common structure before— making distinctions and part/whole systems. They are quick to engage because its familiar terrain, even though the content is totally unrelated, the structure is the same as the ones they saw in their pre-K classrooms. Children are already starting to use the language of DSRP to describe and elucidate their thinking. Metacognition is apparent at an early age.

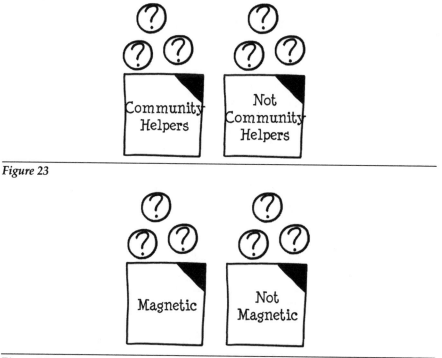

Figure 23

Figure 24

Second graders in Ms. Wilson's class brainstorm objects that are magnetic and not-magnetic (see Figure 24). The topic is different but the common structures are the same (identity/other distinctions and part/whole systems). The teacher uses lots of tactile objects to facilitate the children's construction of abstract thoughts with concrete materials. The students use DSRP to explicitly language their thinking, and they even use the sub-elements of D, S, R, and P (identity/other, part/whole, etc.). They build abstract mental models and match them to real-world objects and phenomena. The common structures are so familiar they're like second nature to them. Children make connections horizontally across topical areas. They're seeing distinctions at home, on the playground, and in their personal relationships.

Ms. Kerry's third-grade class builds off their earlier lessons on the five senses when she guides her students to distinguish between the five senses and how they are similar and different (see Figure 25). Students are then asked to interact with different things (food, flowers, etc.) by using only one sense at a time and then later they are asked to imagine what life would be like without that particular sense. Because they've done this type of work before in earlier grades (same topic and same structure), they begin going beyond the lesson and relating (interaction) the distinctions they made between the senses. Unprompted, students begin to wonder whether the senses influence each other.

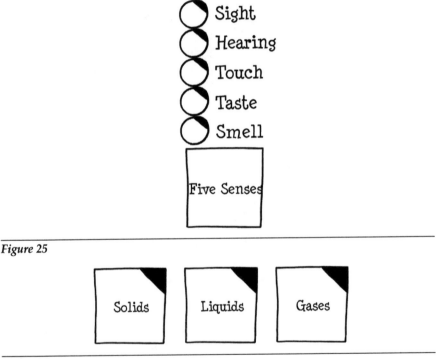

Figure 25

Figure 26

Figure 26 demonstrates a way in which sixth graders learn the differences among solids, liquids, and gases in and of themselves through distinction making. They can further refine their distinction by explicating the many ways they relate to one another (e.g., condensation, evaporation, etc.).

Ninth-grade students distinguish between pH and other forms of measurement (see Figure 27). Then, they compare and contrast acids and bases and understand their differences through their part/whole structure and relationships. The teacher guides the students through building

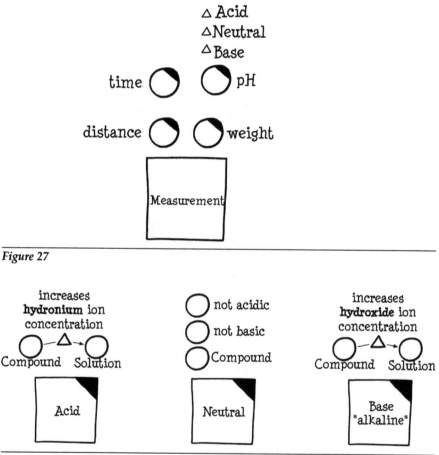

Figure 27

Figure 28

a mental model of the distinction and then gets them involved in working with different real-world acids and bases. After the activity, the students journal in their "knowledge notebooks" by using DSRP diagrams (see Figure 28) to show that they understand the information and the underlying structures.

In a religious studies class, 10th graders build mental models that explore Eastern and Western thought styles along with reading great works of major philosophers. As they read, they build a physical model using blocks and DSRP diagrams in their knowledge notebooks (see Figure 29). Over the course of the semester, they add their own interpretations and build a shared construct to frame their class discussions. Distinguishing between these two major ideas can be both robust and accessible, individual and cooperative when students have a language to discuss their thinking.

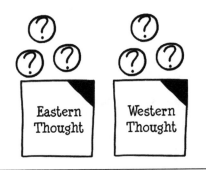

Figure 29

Figure 30

A 12th-grade AP social studies teacher brings current events into the classroom when he asks students to distinguish between two different perspectives on the war in Afghanistan (see Figure 30). Note that perspectives can be distinguished from one another just as simply as any idea or object. By the time students reach the upper grades, their exposure to DSRP allows this to occur seamlessly and effortlessly in any topic. Discussions are more robust, engaged, and richer in detail. The teacher barely needs to facilitate.

CHAPTER THREE

Systems

Every whole has parts. Every part is a whole. Every whole is a part. The parts are in the whole. The whole is in the part. Understand that, and you're on your way to understanding the whole enchilada. The first universal structure we discussed, that of distinctions, allows us to distinguish between different *things* (husband, wife, predator, prey, meat, potatoes, Simon, Garfunkel, and so on). When we distinguish between and among things, we make them different, but when we relate them we make them part of a system. The universal structure discussed in this chapter is systems. The simplest definition of a system is "two or more *related things*." (The universal structure that will be discussed in the next chapter, relationships, says that once *things* are established, we *relate* them [e.g., husband/wife, predator/prey, meat/potatoes, Simon/ Garfunkel].)

Many of the things we can say about making distinctions are true for organizing systems, too. To say that distinctions are all around us is a gross understatement; the same is true of systems. Systems are ubiquitous—they are part of every thought in every moment of every day, no matter the situation. If, simplistically speaking, distinctions are how we name the world, then systems thinking is how we carve it up into parts or lump it together into wholes.

Seeing things as parts and wholes seems like a basic skill, but, like distinction making, it has profound implications for our students. When students see the systemic properties of things, the distinctions they make become more detailed. They see both the coarse- and fine-grained aspects of an idea. They redraw existing boundaries on systems of knowledge, making them aware of the shortsightedness of fixed categorical thinking. They begin to routinely challenge the categorical groupings made in any field and recognize the very perspective from which the grouping originated. Boundaries that once existed in their minds are removed, as the infinite embeddedness of parts and wholes becomes clear. Students see knowledge as it is—fluid and interconnected. Ideas are no longer static facts that exist in isolation; they are seen to be nested and connected with other ideas around them.

Like we did with distinctions, there are some easy ways you can incorporate the metacognition of systems into your classroom. First, it's important to recognize that the systems of part/whole structure are ubiquitous and that this basic structure is universal to many other cognitive operations that are already occurring in your classroom every minute of every day. For example, if you look at the root list of terms for systems structure, you see a pretty common set of cognitive functions:

> group, sort, organize, part/whole, systems thinking, categorizing, hierarchies, tree diagramming, sets, clusters, together, apart, piece, combine, amalgamate, codify, systematize, taxonomy, classify; most words starting with the prefix org- such as organization, organ, or organism; total, sum, entirety, break down, take apart, deconstruct, collection, collective, assemble, type, kind, nature, manner, variety, class, quality, form, bracket, genre, species, family, order, generation, vintage, make, model, brand, stamp, stripe, ilk, cast, grain, mold, categorize, catalog, grade, arrange, order, marshal, systematize, pigeonhole, sort out, arrange, assemble, marshal, put straight, collocate, coordinate, fix up, set up, typecast, stereotype

Of course, we can't get out of bed in the morning without sorting and classifying, organizing, and grouping, never mind attending class. When we awake, there's the alarm clock, the birds, the hum of the house—all of these are sorted in our consciousness as a system of sounds. The alarm clock, the iPhone, and the hair dryer are all electronic. The nighttable, the dresser, and the bed are all classified as furniture. When we get to the shower, there's a system of toiletries that include distinctions such as shampoo, conditioner, soap, body wash, shaving cream, hand cream, body lotion, toothpaste, floss, etc. Breakfast is no different, there are fruits—a part/whole collection of apples, oranges, bananas, and pears. There are cereals, another distinct collection of well-marketed grains. On and on it goes, with each big larger system broken down into smaller and smaller systems. Automobiles can be sorted into cars and truck; trucks into 18 wheelers and pickups; pickups into Toyotas and Fords and Chevrolets. When we get to school, there are any number of part/whole groupings distinguishing who belongs to what and what belongs where. From periods to subject matter to social cliques, our students traverse gracefully (and sometimes not so gracefully) from one part/whole grouping to another. It is, pun intended, part and parcel of the human experience to move into and out of, exist within, and transcend the boundaries of part/whole systems. Minute to minute, day by day, year after year, we live among, inside of, and outside of part/whole systems.

As a teacher, there are some easy ways to get part/whole systems into your classroom, in order to make this powerful and ubiquitous universal structure more metacognitive for you and your students. To give language and expression to that which is already occurring in your classroom. Paying attention to the root list is one important skill so that you will notice part/whole systems as they occur. Another is to use the guiding questions for systems.

Does _____ have parts?

Can you think of _____ as a part?

It bears repeating that guiding "questions" aren't always questions that you literally ask your students. Sometimes you will ask them out loud, but sometimes you'll ask them to yourself and then use your answers to guide your teaching or to better understand what a student is constructing. It makes no difference what subject matter or grade you teach, these guiding questions for part/whole systems are universal:

Does _____ have parts?	Can you think of _____ as a part?
What are the parts of a fire truck? (e.g., cab, engine, ladder)	What is a fire truck a part of? (e.g., community, firehouse, etc.)
What are the parts of the pond ecology? (e.g., flora, fauna, water, minerals, etc.)	What is pond ecology a part of? (e.g., forest ecology, hydrological system, Earth ecology)

What are the parts of a mathematical expression? (e.g., variables, symbols)	What are mathematical expressions a part of? (e.g., mathematical equations, problem solving, etc.)
What are the parts of the Battle of Saratoga? (e.g., Battle of Bemis Heights, Battle of Freeman's Farm)	What is the Battle of Saratoga a part of? (e.g., the Revolutionary War, New York history)
What are the parts of a molecule? (e.g., two or more atoms, covalent bonds)	What are molecules a part of? (e.g., gases, liquids, solids)
What are the parts that make up your concept of torture? (e.g., infliction of pain, relatively long time span, lack of empathy)	What is torture a part of? (e.g., practices of war, methods to illicit information, practices that are illegal under the Geneva Convention)
What are the parts of the DSRP Method? (e.g., distinctions, systems, relationships, perspectives)	What is the DSRP Method a part of? (e.g., cognition, methods for teaching metacognition, methods for structuring information)

Aside from the root list and guiding questions for systems, another great way to begin incorporating systems thinking in your classroom is to use DSRP diagrams. DSRP diagrams are a universal graphic organizer—that means they can be used to organize any information in any grade visually and graphically. Unlike other graphic organizers, such as mind maps, there is also very little cognitive bias in DSRP diagrams, which means that students will bring their own thinking to the content rather than force content into a predetermined structure that may not be the most appropriate for the job. For systems thinking, the diagrams are very simple. We use squares, circles, and triangles. The simple rule is that triangles are parts of circles and circles are parts of squares. So, a part/whole system of any kind will look like Figure 31. In the diagram, you can "read" the diagram as "a whole with three parts, each its own whole having three parts."

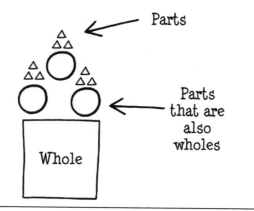

Figure 31

Systems: Part/Whole

When we think of a system, we think of much more than we realize. By implication, we think about the parts of that system and then understand how they relate to form a whole. Thus, the elements of every system are parts and wholes. So we can say that each system is composed of part + whole (see Figure 32).

Systems

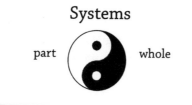

part   whole

Figure 32

All knowledge has part/whole structure; therefore, to understand it, we must see the part/whole structure of each and every idea we encounter. It is easy to see; the universe at every level of scale is organized into a part/whole structure. We cannot grasp any field of knowledge without seeing the part/whole structure of systems. There is no idea in any subject matter that is not made up of parts and wholes. Read this carefully: A system is not a thing; it is a relationship between or among the parts and the whole. There are many types of systems, from physical to conceptual, from the superficial to the salient. Systems can be wildly different from each other, but one thing they have in common universally is their part/whole structure.

Every whole has parts and all parts are wholes. Seeing the part/whole structure simultaneously is a crucial part of organizing systems. Note, too, that "parts and wholes" works much like "identity/other." That is, they are relative to each other. Every part is a whole. And every whole is a part. Seeing that any idea is both a part and a whole is foundational not only to systems thinking, but to all thinking.

These few vignettes—from Russian nested dolls (matryoshka dolls) to ecological systems, as well as everything between and beyond—show that the part/whole structure underlying all bodies of knowledge can't be missed. As your mind becomes more aware of this universal thinking pattern, you will start to see it everywhere and in everything you do.

Seeing Systems

Laura's daughter Gianna was struggling with math homework and asked for help. "Fractions, ugh!" she said. Laura told her that fractions might seem like numbers and math, but really they show up all over the place whenever we break something down into parts. That's because fractions are merely part/whole thinking disguised as math. Gianna was skeptical. (What self-respecting 7-year-old wouldn't be?)

"Bring me something and I'll show you," Laura suggested.

"Like what?" she asked.

"Like anything."

So she brought a ketchup bottle. Laura told her it was a good choice, because even a bottle of ketchup is made up of parts. (In truth, anything she had chosen would have been a great choice, because everything in the universe can be broken into part/whole.) Laura asked Gianna to name all the parts she could isolate. She came up with a good list: a plastic bottle, a cap, two sticker labels, the red stuff (the ketchup itself), and all the ingredients that make up the stuff. She was splitting the whole into parts.

Laura then guided her to isolate any one of those parts to notice that it, too, was made up of parts. She chose the cap. Gianna noted that it was made of plastic, a top and a bottom, a hinge, a hole that lets the ketchup through, a little bump that fits into the hole to seal it shut, and those spirals at the cap's base that let you screw the cap onto the bottle top. "Cool," said Gianna. She had taken a single part, transformed it into a whole, and broken it further into smaller parts. From there, Laura and Gianna looked at the problems with fractions to see how Gianna could transfer her understanding of part/whole to her homework (see Figure 33). She learned that any number or thing could be broken into parts: for example,

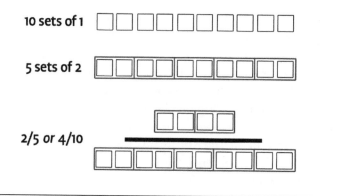

10 sets of 1

5 sets of 2

2/5 or 4/10

Figure 33

10 could be broken into ten 1s. Also, 10 could be broken down in a different way such as five 2s. Depending on how she rendered the parts, the fractions could be different; using Cheerios, or M&Ms, or even little squares, she could see that 2/5 and 4/10 were numerically the same.

That night, Gianna sat up in bed when Laura tucked her in. Laura suspected her daughter was stalling to stave off the inevitable bedtime, but in fact Gianna was inspired. She couldn't stop herself from applying her new understanding of part/whole relationships to her bedroom. "Look, Mom, my room is made of walls, and a ceiling, a rug, a bed, a door. . . . And if you just take the door as a whole, it's made up of its own parts: wood, paint, a doorknob, hinges. . . . And you can take one of those parts as a whole, too, like the doorknob, and it's made of metal, the knob, little screws. . . . You could just keep doing this for everything in the room." Gianna had gotten it completely. We find that she's typical: Children love part/whole thinking and have a lot of fun with it.

The Physical Universe Is Nested In Part/Whole

If only one idea had to be passed on to the next generation, it is the concept of atoms and molecules, and that everything is made of them.
　—Richard Feynman

Gianna relayed the part/whole structure of her room by looking at it in both directions. We can and should do this with any object or idea. We can look "up" and see the whole that something is a part of, and then we can look up again to see a whole that contains that whole as one of its parts. Or we can look "down" and see the parts that make up that something. And we can look down again, and again, to see the parts of the parts.

Early Indian and Greek philosophers thought the universe was made up of indivisible atoms. The word "atom" literally means "not-cuttable": a meaning "not" and tomos meaning "to cut." In the 17th and 18th centuries, chemists offered a physical theory of the atom's indivisibility. But in the 19th and 20th centuries, physicists discovered that the atom has structure and subatomic components. Knowledge changes: The atom is cuttable after all.

On the other end of the spectrum, the word "universe," literally meaning "one whole," was originally chosen to denote "everything." The universe was the whole of wholes. Anything you could think of was part of the universe. The universe was the final whole and was the only whole that didn't serve as a part of anything larger. Wrong again. Knowledge changes. Today, cosmologists, physicists, astronomers, philosophers, theologians, and fiction writers have proposed a multiverse (or meta-universe) that includes multiple universes. It seems our whole universe is merely a partial speck of dust in a much larger metaverse of metaverses. From the subatomic to the super-universal, part/whole structure prevails. From the infinitesimal to the infinite, parts are nested in wholes and those wholes are in turn nested in larger wholes.

A classic toy that exemplifies the nested nature of systems is the matryoshka doll, or the Russian nested doll. "Matryoshka" is a nickname derived from "Matryona," a name in Russian culture that evokes a stout and sturdy woman. These beautiful dolls are cylindrical in shape (tapering just a bit at the neck) and open via a horizontal slit in the middle. Faces, arms, hair or head wraps, and dresses are painted on. The largest doll contains all the others. The child opens her to reveal the next, opens that one to reveal the next, and so on until the "baby" doll (the smallest one) is reached. Each inner doll is a whole that contains another. Each doll is also a part of the whole matryoshka unit.

Figure 34

As educational toys, matryoshka dolls are ingenious, containing within them not only multiple dolls but the potential for true transformative learning. Simply put, it changes children's minds. With a little facilitation, kids handling these dolls will come to know one of the most essential of all principles: The universe itself has a part/whole structure. Matryoshka dolls, and other tools that allow students to physically manipulate part/whole, transform children into splumpers (see page 66).

The Knowledge of the Universe Is Nested in Part/Whole

Although scientists do use deep, analytical methods to determine knowledge structures, such sophistication is hardly required to see what is right before our eyes. For example, if we simply scour an encyclopedia and remove all of its images and line them up in a grid, we can see that despite the diversity of topics and disciplines, each image clearly indicates part/whole structure.

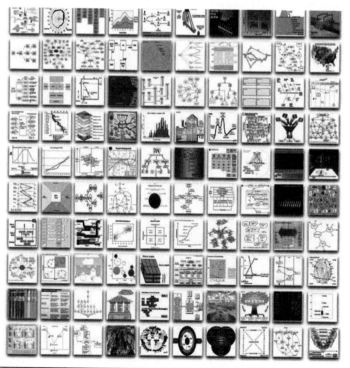

Figure 35

The knowledge we construct is a representation of our real physical universe. It's not perfect—we are always learning more about things and changing what we know—but it is approximate. In other words, although our knowledge is imperfect, there is correspondence between what we know and what is real. It makes sense then that the universal structures we find in knowledge will parallel structures in the universe.*

Splitters and Lumpers Make Splumpers

There's an old saying in science that although there are many types of scientists, there are fundamentally only two kinds of scientists: splitters and lumpers. Splitters are those scientists who reduce the whole into parts, splitting it up into manageable bites for analysis and study. Lumpers are the integrators. They find parts and lump them together. In the 21st century, we need our students and scientists to be splumpers. Gianna is a splumper. Richard Feynman was a splumper. You and your students can be splumpers, too. You need only to think of systems that are part and whole.

As students need to understand knowledge, they must be able to split ideas into component parts *and* lump parts in to new ideas. This act of "splumping" leads to a far deeper understanding of all knowledge and creates thinkers who can solve complex problems with robust solutions. Let's look at some cases from real classrooms to see how splumping is put to use.

Fire Trucks, Lockdowns, and Apples

Ms. Callister was trained in the DSRP Method and recognized right away that her kids were already little DSRP'ers; they just didn't know it yet. She began by teaching her students about systems by explaining to them the relationship between a part and the whole. At the beginning of the year, she explained the idea that every thing (a whole) has parts, and that those whole things are often parts of bigger things. This is the beginning of systems thinking, and part/whole is one of the DSRP structures we teach students easily. She explicitly referenced part/whole during attendance and in other areas of her student's day (lunchtime, nap time, etc.) and then asked the students to use it in more formal lessons.

---

*Schneps, M. (1989). Private universe project: Harvard University. See http://www.thinkingateverydesk.com.

Each year, Ms. Callister taught her 3- and 4-year-olds a standard on "community helpers," one of which is a firefighter. A big fan of hands-on learning, she has a fire truck pull up in the parking lot. Her students then build their own model fire truck out of cardboard.

Ms. Callister has been building fire trucks with her students for many years. But this year, the first year she used DSRP, she noticed some surprising and exciting things that her students did that she had not seen in previous years. As her students began to build the cardboard fire truck, they had begun to include more and more parts than ever before. The students had moved beyond the typical parts (cab, back, steering wheel) to include hoses, the ladder, the different types of doors, mirrors, the oxygen tank, and so on. When Ms. Callister taught her students to always ask "does this part have parts?" they had learned to look further, to see more. They built a model in their heads that looked something like Figure 36. Each child's model was different, of course, but the universal similarity among them was their part/whole structure. Ms. Callister asked penetrating questions and set up situations to constantly elicit more information that would allow her to better understand the structures her children were building in their heads.

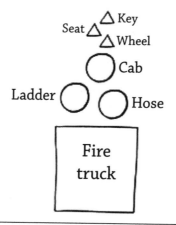

Figure 36

Imagine this. Let's say the children are limited to only what they can accomplish physically. Imagine she asked the kids to go out and *literally* take the fire truck apart with their hands. How successful would they be? Not very . . . maybe they'd manage to get a mirror off. But, what if she gave them some tools, like hammers or screwdrivers, they'd get a few more pieces off the truck, yes? That's all DSRP is doing. It gives kids the explicit *cognitive* tools they need to take things (or ideas) apart and put them back together. That's why these kids are making more distinctions and seeing more parts and parts of parts: They're actually *seeing more*.

Ms. Callister's students took the DSRP structure and ran with it themselves, becoming their own best teachers and transferring their learning to other topics. Several weeks after the fire truck visited, there was a lockdown at Ms. Callister's school. Lockdowns were new to the 3- and 4-year-olds. After the lockdown was over, one girl raised her hand and asked, "Ms. Callister, can we part/whole the lockdown?" And there it is again. Transfer.

The class decided to understand the lockdown by using part/whole structure—for example, "first, we lock the door, then we turn off the lights . . . then we go to the back of the room . . ." In other words, this concept "lockdown" had more meaning for the children once they broke down the whole into parts. Although Ms. Callister's kids did not draw diagrams in this example, we can diagram their constructions as shown in Figure 37 to better understand their thinking.

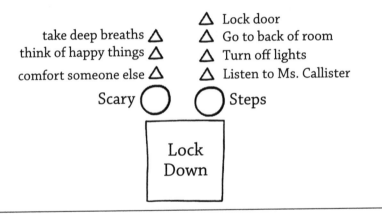

Figure 37

Here again, we would be amazed at this case were it not for the fact that we see it over and over again. This is an example of 3- and 4-year-olds exhibiting far transfer, teaching themselves things, being autodidactic, and demonstrating the skills of lifelong learners and how to be knowledgeable. They took the part/whole structure they had used in the fire truck lesson and then applied it in a novel situation.

If that's not impressive enough, two months later we received an email from Ms. Callister's class. They had just finished a lesson on apples that included a field trip to an apple orchard. As students were deconstructing the parts of an apple, they came across a part that looked different but they didn't know the name for it, so they temporarily named it "the apple's belly button" because the little hole with the "fur" in it reminded them of a belly button. In their email, they wanted to know if we knew the name of the apple's belly button. We didn't. But Cornell has a well-known plant biology department so we forwarded the email message to a colleague who studies plants. It turns out that the name of the apple's belly button is the calyx. Now there are 30 4-year-olds in Virginia who know the word "calyx" and understand it as a part of their apples. What Ms. Callister's kids did was pretty amazing on deeper inspection. They used part/whole structure to create a "placeholder" for a part that they saw in their study of apples. They didn't know they name for it, but they knew it had one and they wanted to find out what it was called. Their use of part/whole guided their self-directed inquiry!

Once again, Ms. Callister's students did not (in this case) use DSRP diagrams, but Figure 38 (which we created) helps to show what exactly happened in their little genius minds. In the first step they simply used the part/whole structure to deconstruct an apple. They added the usual parts and then noticed something that was distinctly different (notice distinctions entering into the process): a "furry part"! At first, they simply added

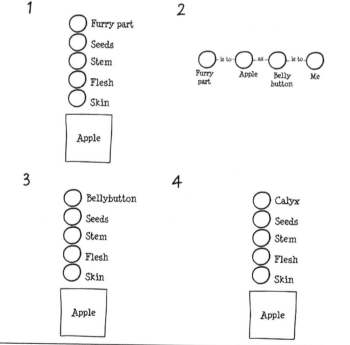

Figure 38

the part as a sort of placeholder for the information they hadn't found yet. In step 2, they made an analogy. The analogy was that the furry part is to an apple as a belly button is to me (notice prior knowledge structures are informing their thinking here). In step 3, the students changed their working distinction from "furry thing" to "belly button." But they weren't satisfied, so they emailed Derek to see if he knew the name of the apple's belly button (notice their rudimentary use of early scientific and research skills coming into play; these are the same research skills used by doctoral students to identify if something is known yet or if it is fertile ground for a novel contribution to the literature). Finally, in step 4, having heard back from us, they added it to their new mental model and vocabulary.

Ms. Callister's students will successfully navigate the rest of their education being armed with a significant advantage: understanding how they think, or metacognition. We see the same types of student experiences occurring in all of our DSRP classrooms. As these students transition from preschool to elementary school to middle school to high school to college, they possess in them an ability that allows them to approach any new area of knowledge they choose to study and eventually work in as adults. That ability is knowledge-ability.

More Examples: Organizing Systems into Parts and Wholes

There are many opportunities to develop part/whole thinking as a skill in students with very little effort in existing curricula. Here are a few examples of lessons in classrooms.

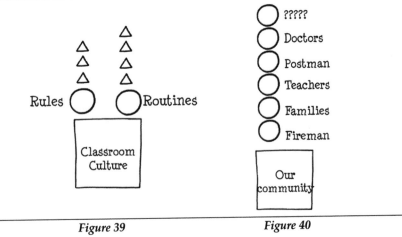

Figure 39   Figure 40

Pre-K students understand the rules and routines of their classroom by breaking it into its parts (see Figure 39). Kindergartners think about the question "who is part of our community?" and discover many parts like firemen, families, teachers, postman, doctors, and so on, and their construct (Figure 40) can be added to and refined over time.

An important idea in early mathematics is the difference between unity and quantity. These two abstract concepts are foundational to the students' later understanding of many other important math concepts such as algebraic equations and variables (in math and other disciplines). To understand the difference in the two ideas—unity and quantity—we must teach students to make a distinction between them (see Figure 41).

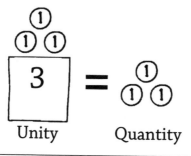

Figure 41

Figure 42

Students then need to understand the relationship between the two ideas—that they are equal in value (e.g., 3) but different in their parts. Whereas a quantity of 3 is represented by three separate 1's, the unity of 3 is a single object (system) made up of three 1's (Figure 42). Understanding this idea early on in their exposure to mathematics opens students up to the more complex equations they will see as they progress in grades. Certainly being able to see (through a diagramming technique) the structural difference by using DSRP co-locates the structure of the ideas with the content of the lesson. This ability to learn the information of a lesson in concert with the thinking processes (DSRP) leads to a true understanding of the lesson and of themselves.

Here are more examples:

- Fourth-grade students in New York deconstructed the Battle of Saratoga into two smaller battles: Freeman's Farm and Beemus Heights (Figure 43). They then recognized that the Battle of Saratoga is a whole with two parts; also, the battle is a part of the larger idea, the American Revolution.

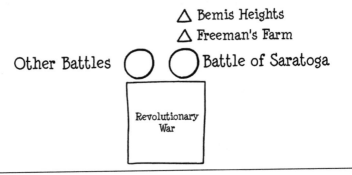

Figure 43

- An English Language Arts class compared different genres of writing based on their part/whole structure (novel, short story, poem, etc.) (Figure 44).

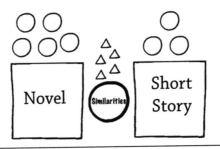

Figure 44

- A student learned about the parts of the American Civil War based on the Northern and Southern perspectives (Figure 45). She also learned the important connection between perspective and the parts we see in any idea. For example, from the Northern perspective, the war was called "the Civil War," whereas Southerners referred to it as "the War of Northern Aggression."

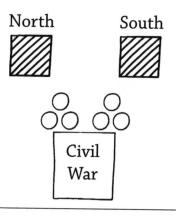

Figure 45

• A sixth-grade math teacher in Virginia saw a student struggling to understand the difference between an expression and equation, but she quickly realized that the DSRP guiding questions might do the trick. Stepping up to the blackboard, she asked, "So what are the parts of an expression?" As the student listed them, she drew a diagram on the board, and then asked the same question of equations, the resultant diagram was Figure 46.

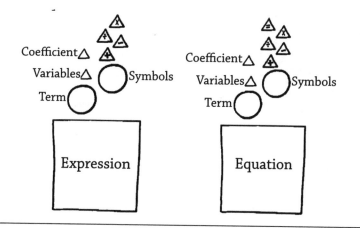

Figure 46

A student deconstructed an abstract mathematical concept into a part/whole structure in order to see the difference between them: in this case, the equals sign and its implications. This simple shift in the teacher's approach to the problem allowed for a much deeper understanding for her student, in less than 5 minutes.

- A middle school science class broke an ecosystem into its biotic (producers, consumers. and decomposers) and abiotic parts (heat, air, water, soil) (Figure 47).

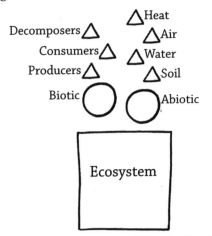

Figure 47

- A high school teacher began his unit on acids and bases with a review of prior knowledge of concepts like atoms, elements, and compounds.

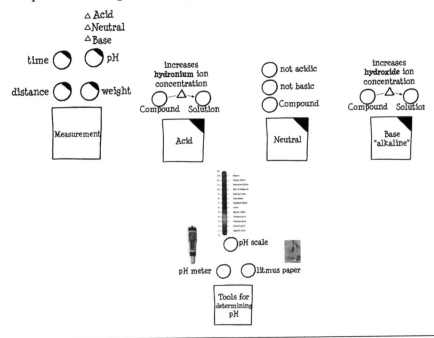

Figure 48

He asked students to identify the parts of each of the ideas, simply by asking, "What are the parts of ___?" about each one. And then "How do they relate to each other?" He focused their attention on compounds, which consist of one or more chemical elements. "What happens to compounds when we put them into solutions?" He explained the basics of pH, the measure of the acidity or basicity of an aqueous solution, and the difference between neutral (a pH close to 7.0 at 25° C, or 77° F), acidic (a pH less than 7), and basic (solutions with a pH greater than 7) (Figure 48). He reflected on the lesson, noting that the part/whole structure was an excellent way to present new information to his students—and it also helped them to relate new knowledge back to their prior knowledge—all in one integrated unit. He checked their understanding of the material through visual DSRP maps and was able to see how they organized the information into part/whole structures and then relate them.

- A teacher from Texas contacted us for advice on how to infuse DSRP into her standards-based lesson, to "separate a whole into 2, 3, 4 equal parts and use appropriate language to describe the parts such as 3 out of 4 equal parts." The teacher taught the lesson content and the thinking skills needed to deconstruct these ideas and build new knowledge for each student by constructing Figure 49. She separated the content

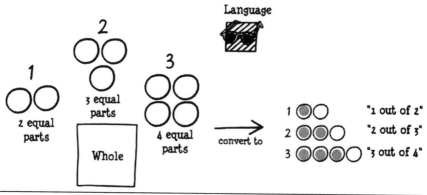

Figure 49

of the lesson, such as the concepts "parts," "whole," "equal," and "descriptive language," and included the following thinking skills:

- to *distinguish* between the whole and its parts (distinction making);
- to explicate the parts of the whole (*systems*);
- *relate* the part/whole system to "appropriate language;" and

- look at the part/whole relationship from the *perspective* of language to teach the kids that one whole with two parts is spoken as "one out of two," and so on.

The phrase *organizing systems* might not conjure up anything terribly meaningful or robust in and of itself in your mind. But, understanding the simple elements of systems—part and whole—is a universal pattern of thinking; all fields of knowledge are systems made up of parts and wholes, whether they are physical and structural or abstract and conceptual. All knowledge has part-whole structure, and therefore to understand it, we must see the part-whole structure of each and every idea we encounter. It is easy to see if we look for it, because at every level of scale the universe is organized into a part-whole structure. We all organize things into systems. We can't help it. The universe provides many opportunities to do so, given that it all contains part-whole structure. All fields of knowledge use systems to self-organize. When students understand that knowledge is structured in parts and wholes relating to one another, they are intuitively given the power to both construct new knowledge or to deconstruct and better understand existing bodies of knowledge. They gain a cognitive foothold into how to analyze and explicate entire systems of thought. Ideas are more easily explored, connected, and nested among a vast array of other ideas.

CHAPTER FOUR

Relationships

Carl Jung wrote, "The meeting of two personalities is like the contact of two chemical substances; if there is any reaction, both are transformed." Jung was making an observation about the deep similarities between two very different subject areas: chemistry and psychology. He saw a common structure in relationships despite the vast chasm between their domains. When two chemical substances react, both are transformed in the same way that when we meet another person, our lives are altered in some small or significant way. This holds true when we make a relationship between two ideas; the meaning of both constructs is transformed. This is the second pattern of thinking: relationships.

Relating ideas is so universal that we cannot make a single distinction without also making a relationship; a distinction is the relationship between identity and other. In turn, once we have a few ideas distinguished from each other, we can begin to relate them. When we do, like Carl Jung said, both are transformed.

In our workshops, we use a simple and powerful exercise to show the way that ideas in a relationship transform one another. We begin by writing the word "coat" and asking a participant to describe it. Usually, participants describe a coat based on the season, so in winter they might say it's warm, brown, and hiplength. Then we present the word "lab" and ask our volunteer to relate the two words and to describe the coat again. Whatever the coat looked like before, it now becomes a long button-up white coat, made of cotton, and with a pocket for pens. Then we add a third word. We put in the word "dog" and ask them to describe the coat again. In an instant, the coat becomes the fur of a Labrador retriever. Of course, what also changed was the person's concept of "lab," which initially was a scientist's laboratory coat and then became a Labrador retriever. This sequence of conceptual transformations elucidates the hidden and universal structure of Relationships: inter + action.

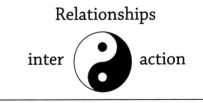

Relationships

inter   action

Figure 50

Figure 50 illustrates an everyday fact about your own classrooms. That is, your students engage with ideas every day and each day any number of ideas are zooming around in their heads crashing into each other, altering each other, and creating new knowledge. If a student is learning a new idea in chemistry about the volatility of bonding molecules having just come from a home where the morning ritual is a mom and dad fighting, that student will be making relationships that other students won't be. The student might construct not only new knowledge about chemistry but also new knowledge about human social dynamics. Likewise, the pubescent boy three seats over who's pining for the girl two seats up may be constructing another construct, similar to but different from what the teacher is teaching or what the previous boy had thought. As a teacher, understanding what your students are constructing is not only important, but it's also the very definition of teaching and learning. Teaching is not merely knowing in front of people but knowing what your students are constructing and helping them be aware of those constructions so that they can guide their own learning.

Many of our teacher trainees find that our "root lists" for DSRP are helpful to understand not only how universal each of the four parts of DSRP are (you're doing them all the time), but also how often you are already teaching relationships in your classroom. The following root list for relationships shows us that understanding DSRP is not about incorporating a "new" educational framework into your classroom: DSRP is already happening in your classroom. The DSRP Method merely gives us a language for thinking and an awareness of our thinking (metacognition). Relationships—a basic, foundational pattern of thinking—lie at the core of all of these types of activities:

connect, relate, interconnection, interaction, link, cause, effect, affect, rank, leads to, results in, because, subsequently, attach, join, hitch, stick, adhere, associate with, partner; affiliate, align, join, ally, merge, integrate, mingle, socialize, network, joint, association, bond, tie, attachment, fasten, bind, unite, combine; most words with the prefixes inter-, intra-, extra-, such as interdisciplinary, intramural; between, among, feedback, couple, associate; most words with the prefix co- as in coupling, couple, couple with; colleague, coworker, connection, contact, collaborator, correlate, cooperate, communicate; types of relationships such as linear, nonlinear, causal, feedback, and mathematical operators such as +, -, /, and x; any phrases ending in with or to, such as link to/with, empathize with, get on well with, etc.; also common social interactions like "friending," "liking," etc., are all forms of relationships—linkages between one thing and another

Relationships are universal to our thinking. We make relationships of one sort or another every second of every day. So do your students. This is why the guiding questions are so useful, because they are so universal. The guiding questions for R are as simple as those for D, S, and P are, but because they are universal, having them in your teacher's tool belt will extend the range of your discussions, help you to help your students penetrate and engage their own thinking, and generally get things flowing in the classroom:

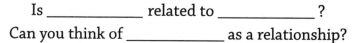

Is _____ related to _____ ?

Can you think of _____ as a relationship?

The first guiding question for R is the most basic. It simply asks, "Is thing A related to thing B?" Of course, things A and B could be anything. Two ideas, two objects, two sports, two wars, two molecules, two words, two novels, two people, two poems, and so on. Here, we are asking about the relationship *between* things. But we could also ask about the relationships *among* things. That means the relationships among three or more things. As teachers, if we get in the habit of asking these R questions all the time, we get our kids thinking about the things they don't know yet.

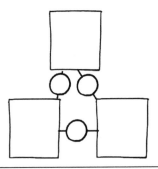

Figure 51

We might be discussing three things such as the three branches of government: executive, legislative, and judicial. But what are the relationships among these three things (see Figure 51)? We know there must be three such relationships, right?

Guiding questions are very useful because they allow teachers, students, and parents alike to ask questions that take us beyond the information we are being given. It's often as easy as counting the number of objects you've been given. For example, if you are discussing two objects or ideas, there is at least one relationship between each of them. If there are three objects or ideas, there must be at least three relationships among them. If there are four objects or ideas, then there must be at least six relationships among them. Five objects or ideas means that there are at least 20 relationships that could be considered, and so on. The simple formula for determining how many relationships might be considered among n objects or ideas is $n*(n-1)/2$. So if we have 6 objects or ideas, using our formula we can see that $6*(6-1)/2 = 6*(5)/2 = 30/2 = 15$. What if we have 20 objects or ideas? $20*(20-1)/2 = 20*(19)/2 = 380/2 = 190$ relationships!

Of course, you probably are not going to explore that many relationships within a class period but it is very powerful to give your students the capability to understand and ask questions about the hidden relationships that might exist between or among ideas or objects. When we give them these tools, they learn to ask questions that penetrate beyond the ideas they are learning, and we teach them to create a connected knowledge base in their own minds. A connected knowledge base is a flexible one, an adaptive one. That will serve students well when they need to use some of what they have learned in a new setting to solve a novel problem.

The second guiding question for R is "Can you think of _____ as a relationship?" Teachers sometimes get confused by this question but it's really very simple and can lead to profound learning opportunities.

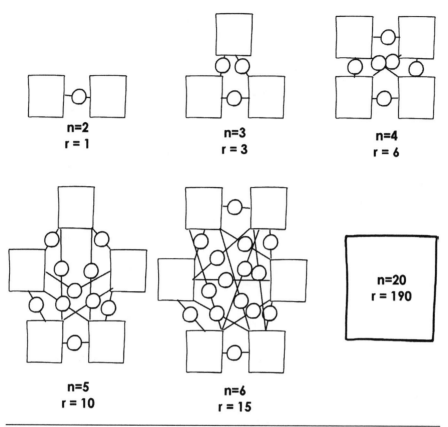

Figure 52

Any idea or object not only has the potential to be related to any other idea or object (that's the basis for the first guiding question) but also any idea or object can be the relationship that is between two other ideas or objects. For example, take the idea of marriage. We can use the first guiding question to ask whether there is a relationship between marriage and society. By using the second question, we might ask, what is marriage a relationship between? The answer could be many-fold. One answer is that marriage is the relationship between husbands and wives. When we see ideas and objects not merely as distinct identities (D) or as whole systems (S), but also as potential relationships between or among other ideas or objects (R), we begin to connect our knowledge in deep and meaningful ways. We are not merely becoming information-full (where we possess a list of unrelated facts and figures); instead, we become knowledge-able (where information is supported by a semantic and cognitive web, a network of meaningful connections).

Of course, you and your students are *already* making relationships in the classroom all the time. Here again, the purpose of the DSRP Method is not to have you add yet another framework to your pedagogical arsenal. Instead, it is to give you and your students and colleagues a language and a method for elucidating and communicating about the thinking that is already occurring in your classroom. This act alone will lead to more metacognitive students (and teachers), higher transfer rates, and deep understanding.

We all relate things. We relate to one another. We understand our own identity based on those that we are related to—the people around us. All fields of knowledge are created by establishing relationships between and among ideas, disciplines, or entire areas of study. We make connections, associations, and links all the time; at the foundation of each of these is the hidden structure of relationships. The following examples range from superfluous to serious, but they illustrate four key points about relationships:

- They are universal.
- They are often hidden or implicit.
- They are distinct and often are systems themselves made up of parts.
- They are inter-relationships (i.e., they go two ways) between and among ideas.

Discovering Hidden Connections

Nature rarely reveals her secrets, especially when it comes to how things are related. When we look at nature it's often easy to see distinct objects or animals, an individual plant or tree, or an entire ecological system like a pond or a greenhouse. It's easy to see the parts of a bridge or a building or distinguish between snowflake crystals or cloud formations. What's really difficult is seeing that which is invisible—the relationships that exist between and among the visibly different parts.

Using the guiding questions is a great way to get your students to ask about relationships that may not be explicit. Another way is by using diagrams or tactile manipulatives like DSRP Blocks (discussed later in this chapter). When a student uses DSRP diagrams or tactile manipulatives to build his or her knowledge, it is much easier to see the objects or ideas and therefore much easier to contemplate the relationships between those ideas or objects. For example, if we give students a diagram with three objects on it, we want them to automatically think of the following:

- "Those three things could have relationships."
- "Are the relationships important to me for the purpose of what I am doing right now?"
- "What might they be?"
- "How many of them are there?"

And so on. Doing these kinds of activities early on in the students' development of explicit thinking skills will lead to lasting and powerful effects. When a student reads an article, is exposed to an advertisement, watches a political ad, or sees a product in a store, they might ask these questions, respectively:

- "What's the relationship between the author of the article and the topic?" (e.g., the author is biased because he owns stock in the company he is promoting)
- "What's the relationship between this product and its claims?" (e.g., the causal claims the product makes to outcomes are spurious and weak)
- "What's the relationship between this political ad and the music choices that were made?" (e.g., the dark and demonic music and awkward images of the candidate together are intended to make me distrust him)
- "What's the relationship between this product and its product placement at the end cap of the aisle?" (e.g., is this product getting better promotion because the company has paid for the promotion or because it's a popular and reliable product bought by many consumers?)

There are ideas and objects being related for us all around us. It is absolutely critical that we help students be metacognitive about the relationships they are making so that they're not simply making the ones marketeers, political operatives, and manipulators want them to make. When we teach our students to see relationships as an explicit part of their thinking, we teach them to see with their mind's eye what they cannot see with the naked eye.

Take a look at the cells in Figure 53. You can see the cell walls, the nucleus, and the plasma, but you cannot see the relationships between and among those parts of the cells. Now imagine that you have been teleported to an unfamiliar dinner party. You can see individual guests but you cannot see the relationships among them. Would you think differently if you knew they were all employees of the same company? Family

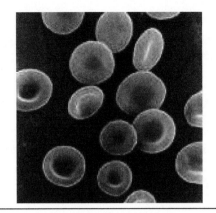

Figure 53

members? Teachers? Relationships matter. The relationships between and among things determine the dynamics of a situation or system. The tricky part is that these incredibly important relationships are often totally invisible. To survive and thrive in the world, we must understand the reality of what's going on, but we're not seeing the whole picture. Without making the invisible relationships visible, our understanding of the world, problems, situations, events, organizations, and people is incomplete.

Because relationships are so often invisible, we must have cognitive reminders to help us make them more visible, more explicit. DSRP in general, specifically R, will act as cognitive reminders. R reminds us to look for relationships where none have been specified and to question relationships (by further deconstructing them with D, S, and P) that have been made explicit. We must ensure that students are making these connections so they can build new knowledge. And when students recognize existing connections, they gain a deeper understanding of what they are studying.

To engage students, a teacher must know the students for who they are. To know them, a teacher must not only understand the distinctions they are making but also the invisible relationships that influence the meaning that they make. Because children are constantly relating ideas, objects, events, people, feelings, thoughts, and so on (often without acknowledging them), teachers must be aware of the influences that these relationships have on children's thinking and understanding. A child often does not know that she has arrived at a particular conclusion because she related one event to another (even if the two events were not related). A great teacher can see that the sideways glance, the introspective head nod, the inquisitive eyebrow raise, and the stubborn arm cross are not physiological twitches but instead are cognitive ideas. The great teacher not only hears what students say but knows that their words communicate only a fraction of their thoughts. The great teacher pieces it all together to come to an understanding of each child's mind. The great teacher comes up with an instantaneous hypothesis: "Elena doesn't understand the importance of the Battle of Saratoga in the Revolutionary War because she's missing the relative power of France to the then-fledgling United States." The teacher then tests the hypothesis and uses it to ask a more penetrating question: "Elena, what do you think the relationship between France and the United States was during the Revolutionary War, and how is it distinctly different from their relationship today?" Now the teacher has Elena thinking about the influence that a relationship has on the distinctions we make.

It is equally important that the teacher helps the child to see the many potential relationships that exist between ideas. But how do we guide students to see them? Here's one simple example that will have dramatic effects. Worksheets that ask students to relate selected items are ubiquitous in schools. Typically, the child is given a worksheet that has several images or words with the assignment to relate the items by drawing a line from one to another. When the child draws the line, we know that he has constructed a relationship but we know very little about what that relationship is in the child's mind. To understand the child's constructions, we need only to ask two simple questions. Let's take a look. Say the child finds "mom" and "dad" on a worksheet and draws a line between them (see Figure 54).

Mom ———————— Dad

Figure 54

What does this line tell the teacher? Not much. We know that the child intuits (or has guessed) that there is a relationship between Mom and Dad, but we don't know what his construct is for that relationship. By combining distinction-making with recognizing the relationship, we can ask the student to name the relationship. This tells us what his concept of the relationship is: Naming the relationship establishes its identity for the teacher and the student. If a student labels the relationship "marriage" or "love" or "me" or "fight a lot," we gain powerful insight into his thinking (see Figure 55).

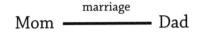

marriage

Mom ———————— Dad

Figure 55

Once the relationship has an identity (such as marriage) we then ask a second question based on systems thinking: What are the parts of marriage? As a student identifies the parts of the relationship, teachers see the child's construct of the idea of "marriage." When students relate two ideas, name the relationship, and explore its parts, the teacher can see how the students are thinking. If we are what we think, then the teacher is getting a window seat into the child's mind. By prompting the child, you will see his own thinking and be more capable of seeing its value or correcting it when necessary.

Interrelationships Lead to Interdisciplinarity

When we relate things, we make new knowledge. Knowledge becomes more interconnected. As students find more relationships among ideas, this increases interdisciplinarity, transfer of learning, analogical thinking, creativity and innovation, and the ability to form new ideas by combining disparate pieces of prior knowledge (see Figure 56). Another way of saying this will make perfect sense: The more we relate things, the more things are related. It is these interrelationships that increase our interdisciplinarity (because that's all interdisciplinarity is—making interrelationships between disciplines). The more we relate things, the more creative we are because creativity is being aware of or seeing connections that others don't. The more we relate things, the more we can transfer them because the ability to transfer is based on the ability to make connections between otherwise seemingly different domains. In other words, the more connections we make, the smarter we get. DSRP helps you see the possibilities in any type of knowledge so you can make more connections. If we had a dollar for every time that a teacher stopped us or emailed us to say, "Is it weird that I feel smarter since using DSRP?" we would be ready to buy a private island.

We need graduates who can make relationships explicit in the course of solving difficult problems that we face in this interconnected world. It makes no difference whether students are 5 or 85 years old—

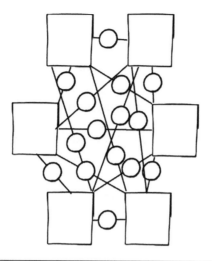

Figure 56

prompting them with guiding questions to see invisible relationships (and distinctions) will deepen their content knowledge and make them more sophisticated thinkers at any age and in any topic. In turn, they'll be invited to the table—to be part of the team that solves the world's most pressing problems and makes society a better place.

Here's a real-world example of how seeing a new relationship not only led to new knowledge but also began a whole new discipline. Before it was recognized as a discipline, biochemistry began as informal relationships among various types of formally trained people. Chemists, biologists, physiologists, immunologists, physicists, and botanists—all curious about the chemistry of biological processes—began to talk and share information. Over time, as scientists engaged with each other, the relationships grew and grew. Scientists began to distinguish biochemistry as a separate but related identity of its own. Today biochemistry is a field of its own. It is no longer just an invisible relationship between biology and chemistry. Biochemistry has its own publishing venues, its world-renowned scholars and experts, its exclusive conferences, and its own accruing body of literature. In short, it has taken on a life of its own. It even has its own perspective, so that someone might approach a problem by asking, "What do the biochemists think of this?"

The birth of biochemistry—from an emerging relationship to a distinct field of knowledge and a complex system of scholars, journals, and conferences—shows us no less than the future of science; which lies in our combining any two (or more) disciplines. Each combination holds new potential because it addresses something that isn't yet addressed by current fields of study. Currently, 20,000 named disciplines of knowledge exist. Out of these, there are 199,990,000 new disciplines that we could hypothetically create based on all the possible paired combinations (not to mention combinations of threes and fours). We've only begun to harvest the possibilities with the likes of econophysics, astrobiology, evolutionary psychology, information technology, and even bioinformatics (the application of information technology to the field of molecular biology).

Each time a new "hybrid" discipline comes into being, it follows a similar process. First, two fields exist and are distinctly different. Someone begins—or, more likely, a few people begin—to relate them to each other. The relationship is implicit at that point. When the relationship grows and begins to have component parts—when it starts to develop into a system—then it is acknowledged as something in itself as opposed to existing as a relation of two other fields. Then it is named and comes into being as a distinction, which encourages further development of its function as a system, and on it grows.

This remarkable process—relationships evolving into a system that solidifies into a distinction with its own perspective—not only births new fields but actually creates permanent changes in our way of perceiving things. It creates true paradigm shifts. We can only begin to imagine the new fields coming in the future and the impact they will have on our research, our technologies, and our lives.

Building New Knowledge

If the value of relating two disciplines to form a new one isn't enough to elucidate the sublime importance of relationships, consider that the very same processes described above are also occurring constantly between individual ideas on a much shorter time span. Creativity and innovation, the creation of new knowledge and new ideas, and the epiphany that leads to the next million-dollar invention follow the exact same processes: relationship, distinction, system.

There are three ways to innovate. First, you can invent something totally new. That's not easy to do. Second, you can make an existing thing better. That takes some skill. Third, you can relate two existing things in a new way. That's an algorithm for creativity and innovation that's used again and again by inventors and entrepreneurs. It involves recognizing a relationship between two products or services that no one else has put together before, such as putting minimarts into gas stations or combining a cell phone and email.

Let's look at the birth of an idea that has changed an entire field of knowledge, and not just any field. Design. This is the field that is responsible for every piece of technology you and your students use, from your laptop to your cell phone to your car or your hair dryer. The spark for the idea that changed the world was simple: It was borne of a relationship. There was a time, not long ago, when designers saw their job as designing a thing—a cell phone or a toaster. Today, the new field of interaction design has changed how designers think about designing. "Designers of digital technology products no longer regard their job as designing a physical object—beautiful or utilitarian—but as designing our interactions with it."*

But it wasn't always called interaction design. Bill Moggridge described his first presentation on the topic at a conference. With the distinction still fuzzy, he called it "'soft-face,' thinking of a cross between software and user-interface design."** Because Cabbage Patch dolls with their mushy faces were ubiquitously popular at the time, a friend of his convinced him to find a name that didn't evoke that image. Thus, the term "interaction design" came to be. He created it with Bill Verplank, another pioneer in the field, who wrote, "As there was not yet any education in interaction design . . . by the end of the eighties, we were starting to feel that we had momentum, and that we could declare ourselves to be interaction designers."***

Interaction designers are important to us. They're the ones who are going to make it possible for an elderly person to use email and for you to connect your classroom to classrooms around the world. They're going to make us sit more comfortably in our chairs, avoid carpal tunnel in our wrists, or safely drive and chat on the phone at the same time. Their work touches all of our lives every day. The spark of genius that made it all possible was seeing a relationship between two things that no one had seen

---

*Moggridge, B. (2007). *Designing interactions*. Cambridge, MA: MIT Press. This quote comes from the front matter of the book, on the first page of text that precedes even roman numeral pagination. It is not written by the author and no other author is named.
**Ibid., 26.
***Ibid., 14.

before. That little relationship changed Bill Moggridge's life and it's still changing our lives.

Implants or Inoculations

When relationships aren't stated explicitly, it often behooves us to bring them to light and name them. Nowhere is this more important than in the way we receive media presentations, whether from news or advertisements or propaganda put out by any organization. Anyone presenting any idea with a motive (whether good or bad or anything in between) is likely to create and put forth relationships between concepts—and these are often left implicit.

We cannot question our thoughts if the relationships we draw remain invisible. Worse, we cannot question what is handed to us by others if we allow the relationships they draw to remain invisible. Consider the work that goes into creating implicit relationships in business or politics. A single marketing executive or political operative (or their teams), armed with great understanding of human thought processes, can construct a single campaign designed to manipulate hundreds, thousands, or even millions of people to do, buy, or vote for something. They take a great deal of time to craft invisible relationships to present in a speech, in an ad, or on a flier. We often take only seconds to receive what they create.

During those seconds, as thinking individuals, we must look for invisible relationships. We must make those relationships explicit for ourselves. We must teach our children and students to make relationships explicit, too. Our task is to determine what relationship exists (or is being posited) in the ideas that we encounter. From there we can ask, "Is it valid?" "Is it true?"

If our own thoughts are not visible, then they're not our own thoughts; they are thoughts given to us by design. An unthinking populace is dangerous because the many can be manipulated to the ends of the few. Implying that a relationship exists between two ideas is a powerful tool used to manipulate us for our money, votes, or attention. Relationships are often implicit, and it is crucial that we recognize them. The simple act of recognizing an implicit relationship that has been made for us, therefore, serves as an inoculation against these manipulations. So, this second pattern of thinking—recognizing relationships—is another seemingly simple task that has profound implications for our children, ourselves, and society. The following cases demonstrate the ease of teaching relationships in various classrooms and topics.

Case Examples

Number Line

All elementary students are introduced to the number line as a strip of paper that looks something like this:

1 2 3 4 5 6 7 8 9 10 11 12 13 14 15 16 17 18 19 20 21 22 23 24

This is a very useful tool for visually remembering the order in which numbers sit on that line. It teaches students that numbers are fixed points on the line, and it reveals nothing about the differences among the numbers, the relationships among the numbers, or the deeper meaning of the organizational structure of this concept we call a "number line." The students' interaction with this line is similar to memorizing spelling words on a list. We want students to see the thinking behind the number line, not to simply recall it.

When we change our approach to teaching by using the DSRP Method, a teacher knows to go beyond the content of the number line by encouraging students to consider how they think about the line. A teacher could simply ask, "Tell me about this number line. What do you see? Why are the numbers organized the way that they are? Is there a reason 12 comes before 13? What is the relationship between 12 and 13?" Asking these types of simple questions encourages students to see that the numbers rest on the line in relation to one another—that 12 is "less than" 13, and 13 is "more than" 12. Thus, they should understand the structure of the line gives the numbers meaning as seen in Figure 57.

Figure 57

On the surface, this simple change in the framework of inquiry may seem innocuous, but it is not. It is one of the first steps in a child's robust understanding of numbers and their relation to each other. More important, it leads to a deeper understanding of the lesson content and develops higher-order thinking, such as how to tell the differences and relationships among the numbers and how these create the number line—which is a system of numbers existing in a part/whole structure. When these same skills—distinguishing, relating, organizing, and taking perspectives on ideas—occur in many lessons in many subjects, students will apply their new skills more efficiently and effectively to all new knowledge as they encounter it year after year. That is the foundation of both vertical and horizontal articulation.

Art

Last year, an art teacher taught her third graders a lesson on Frida Kahlo, her artistic techniques, and the place she was from. She started the lesson by having the students describe the artist, the place she lived, and her artistic techniques. Once students deconstructed the three main ideas in the lesson, she asked them to explicate the relationships among the three: artist, place, and technique. The students' construct looked like Figure 58.

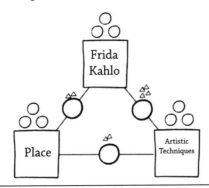

Figure 58

Fast-forward a few months. Now, those third graders were in fourth grade. The teacher used a similarly structured lesson plan to teach about a different artist, Jasper Johns. The DSRP diagram looked like Figure 59.

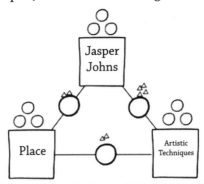

Figure 59

When the class of fourth graders came into the room and saw what the new group of third graders was doing, an interesting thing happened. There was a flash of recognition. The teacher explained, "One of my fourth-grade students noticed the third-grade Jasper Johns artist construct today and she said, '"Oh, the third graders are doing what we did, except we learned about Frida Kahlo!' It is amazing how the student recognized the construct and made that quick connection."

This is one of the great values of helping students see common structures in knowledge. By re-using the same *shape* of an idea, in spite of the difference in content, students are able to transfer learning from one scenario to another.

Now, imagine that same student learning about the three branches of government. If that student were attuned to the structure of ideas (and not just the content), she would see a deep connection between art class and history class (if she used a construct like the one shown in Figure 60). And that would make it easier to understand the new idea being taught in history class. This recognized commonality of DSRP structures is what we strive for—it makes transfer easier. It means learning one thing and then using it in 100 places, not learning 100 things and using them in 100 places.

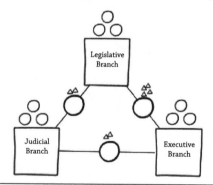

Figure 60

Ocean Geology

In an ideal world, every teacher would be transparent about what the desired learning is, making "framing it" an essential aspect of pre-teaching. "Frame it" means that the teacher needs to know what he or she wants to teach (both the content and the structure). Notice in the diagram in Figure 61 that, first, the teacher would list the distinct parts of ocean geology. These are the nine basic "vocabulary" words that are the main thrust of the assignment. But, if you also want to understand the relationships and perspectives of each, you would ask, "How are these parts related?" and then draw a side-view diagram of the nine elements and how they are related to each other.

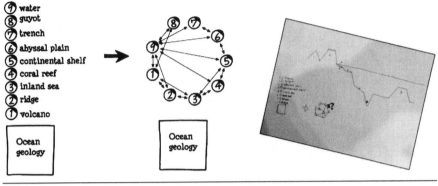

Figure 61

Framing this lesson with a DSRP diagram took less than 5 minutes to think through. Now, students are ready to think about how to take this abstract conceptual learning and transform it into a real-world lesson, where a teacher makes the abstractions more concrete, less conceptual, and more visual, tactile, experiential, and real. The simplest way to reify something is to make it visual, create a metaphor or analogy, or model it with simple physical items (sugar packets, marbles, peas, jelly beans, etc.). The continuum expands into more and more elaborate "reifications" like the one described herein, other more elaborate physical models, games and initiatives, field trips, or complex experiential "rites of passage" like Outward Bound—all are merely reifications of various abstract conceptual ideas. In this example, physical geology allows for a near perfect clay analog model. The side view and top view (a great next step would be to show contour lines on this model) show relief and relationships. This clay model (see Figure 62) includes the elements of blue water, ridge, volcano, shallow inland sea, coral reef, continental shelf, abyssal plain, trench, and guyot.

Students can take the abstract mental model outlined in the DSRP diagrams and make it real by making it experiential (i.e., eyes-on, hands-on, or brain-on in the form of metaphors). Again, reifying need not take a long time or be expensive—metaphors and visual diagrams are free and quick. This model was built in under an hour with a $4 block of clay and a $2 Tupperware (both could be reused) and was a lot of fun. It could easily be built by the teacher in front of the class or by the students. Before the lesson is over, the teacher should take time to check for understanding.

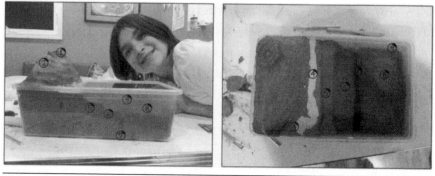

Figure 62

In this lesson, the teacher converted the experience back into an abstract conceptual structure that was flexible, adaptable, and could be re-constructed (not re-membered) by the students at any time in the future. In this step, it's important to see what the students actually constructed as a result of the lesson. After this lesson, one of the kids said, "Oh, I didn't know they were related! I thought they were just stuff." This is a great indication of the difference in constructions between one child and another. Look at the images in Figure 63. The images on the left are models built by children that did not account for relationships whereas the model at right increases the distinctions between the elements because of the relational nature of the model. We can see very easily which child has a better understanding. Having students draw DSRP diagrams is a great way to check for understanding.

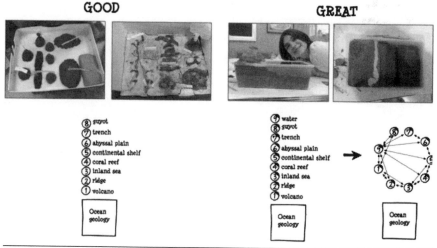

Figure 63

Here are a few more examples of teachers embedding the skill of recognizing relationships into their existing lessons:

A 1st grade class relates the five senses to the appropriate sensory organs.

A 2nd grade teacher has her students look for similarities between novels and short stories.

A 4th grade teacher illustrates the two-way relationships between the states of matter.

A 7th grade teacher helps her science class better understand the human body by explicitly relating the distinct systems (respiratory, skeletal, muscular, pulmonary, nervous) to one another.

When students recognize the implicit relationships between and among ideas, they are more creative, innovative, and flexible in their problem solving skills.

CHAPTER FIVE

Perspectives

The other day a snail got mugged by two turtles (yes, turtle crime is on the rise). The police rushed to the scene of the crime and asked the bewildered snail what had happened.

"I don't know," said the snail. "It all happened so fast."

How long did it take you to laugh? A few seconds? Your brain is remarkable. In order to get this joke, you had to take three perspectives in an instant. First, you understood the idea of speed from the perspective of a snail, then speed from the perspective of a turtle, and finally, your own perspective on speed as a human being. Your brain, as an efficient, perspective-taking machine, took three perspectives within a second. It even does it without us knowing that we needed to do it in the first place! Your mind sorted through three perspectives and put them together in a flash, causing you to laugh. If the process were mapped in an image, it would look like Figure 64.

$$v = \frac{x}{t}$$

Figure 64

Jokes aside, perspective taking—the fourth universal structure—is universal to all thoughts and exists in the knowledge we interact with every day. It also has great importance in our society; it lies at the root of all prosocial behavior such as empathy and compassion. Societies would not survive without perspective. Beyond that, bias, mind-set, stereotypes, paradigms, mediation, negotiation, lock-in, scale, context, and worldview are all based on perspective. It follows then that an ability to make perspectives explicit increases creativity, innovation, conflict-resolution skills, and prosocial behavior for children and adults. Using DSRP diagrams to map perspectives is really easy. We use a symbol of "hash marks" to make the shape being used look like it is a mirror, like the thing is standing in a mirror and is being reflected in the mirror perspective. For example, the example above of the joke can be easily diagrammed (see Figure 65). This is called a perspective circle—a circle of perspectives around a given idea or object. It's a tremendously powerful "common structure," similar in its use to an analogy—something you can use over and over again regardless of the content or topic you are thinking about. Like analogies, you will see perspective circles in use all the time. We'll cover a number of them in this chapter. Being more aware of them will make this an invaluable tool.

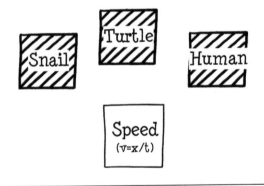

Figure 65

Like distinctions, systems, and relationships, perspective taking isn't something new or a new framework that you need to incorporate into your teaching. Perspective taking is something that you and your students are already doing all the time! Here again, it bears repeating, the purpose of DSRP is not to add another pedagogical framework to your already long list of things to do. The purpose of DSRP is to give a language and a method for what you are already doing and to encourage you and your students to do more of it. Purposefully. Explicitly. To be metacognitive about it.

To become more aware of the perspective taking you are already doing and to motivate you to do more of it, we use several things. First, we start with the basic root list—a list of similar ideas for which perspective taking is the cornerstone. It's by no means a complete list but it will get you started seeing just how much, how often, and how important perspective taking is occurring:

> point of view, point, view, viewpoint, see, look, standpoint, reference point, frame, framework, feeling, angle, interpretation, frame of reference, examination, study, inspection, observation, scan, survey, look-see, onceover, outlook, position, angle, attitude, way of looking at, as in X, in terms of y, aspect, approach, opinion, frame of mind, empathy, compassion, negotiation, scale, mind-set, stance, paradigm, worldview, bias, dispute, context, stereotypes, prosocial behavior, emotional intelligence, dispute resolution, reconciliation; pronouns such as he, she, it, I, me, my, her, him, us, and them

Perspective taking is so powerful, so universal, and so basic a skill that spending the time to show how everything students are learning in every grade and every topic includes perspectives is an essential part of teaching (and learning). Like distinctions, systems, and relationships, the guiding questions we use for perspectives are very helpful in getting teachers (and their students) started in being more metacognitive of perspective taking. Here are the guiding questions for perspectives:

From the perspective of _____ , [insert question]?

Can you think about _____ from a different perspective?

The first question essentially adds a perspectival prefix to any question you can think of.

- From the perspective of clothing, what do we need in winter, spring, summer, or fall?
- From the perspective of shape/color/feelings, what do you see in the piece of artwork?
- From the perspective of quadratic functions, how would you solve this mathematical problem?

The second question "Can you think about _____ from a different perspective?" is similar to the first but asks the students to think of the new point of view that will be taken. Here are a few examples of this question in use:

- Can you think about this pond from a different perspective? (as a frog, duck, turtle)
- Can you think about your dispute from another person's perspective?
- Can you think about the American Civil War from a European perspective?

Like all the four universal structures of thinking, perspectives can be hidden. Sometimes we simply lose track of them, forgetting that we used them to arrive at a particular conclusion in the first place (like the snail joke). When this happens, we risk getting into a sort of bias cul-de-sac, which hinders our ability to "see" what's really going on. Like distinctions, relationships, and systems, perspectives are simple and sublime.

Take a Point and a View

We often think that we have a point of view. We do. But we often miss a critical point of understanding about perspective. A perspective is comprised of a point and a view. The point is the subject, or the position from which the idea is viewed; the view is the object, or what is viewed. Because the point affects the view and vice versa, we expand what we know about any idea in profound ways when we become conscious of both point and view. A point of view is not a static thing; it is actually the relationship between two structural elements: perspectives = point + view (see Figure 66).

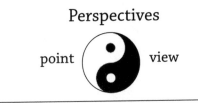

Perspectives

point — view

Figure 66

Taking a perspective is viewing the world or anything in it from a particular point of view. There are physical perspectives, anthropomorphic perspectives, and conceptual perspectives. While we are used to thinking of different people as having differing perspectives, note that every idea has its own perspective as well. Anything we think about, we look at through the perspective or lens of another idea, or a conceptual perspective. In other words, we always look at one idea through another idea. Consider the "Civil War" or the "War between the States": These names reflect the Northern perspective and carry the connotations of a nation divided, torn apart, brother versus brother. Consider the Southern perspective on the very same war. They called it the "war of Northern aggression," which has a different connotation, where the Northern states are seen as the instigators of the war. Teaching our students to see an idea from many perspectives shows them that how we name things, and the parts we see of an idea, are the results of the perspective from which we view the idea.

When you have both a point and a view, you have a perspective. There is no considering or thinking about anything without standing at a point from where we view it. As with any relationship, the point affects the view and the view in turn affects the point; they impact and change each other.

A Change in Perspective Changes Everything

We can look at the same thing (or concept) from different perspectives to magnify its various aspects. Then we come to understand it better. The painting *The Starry Night*, by Vincent Van Gogh, is shown in Figure 67 from various perspectives. We can look at the painting in terms of shape; in terms of line; and in terms of color.

Figure 67

Taking different perspectives is something teachers can do with students from pre-K to PhD. An innovative elementary teacher added another perspective: feelings. So students zeroed in on elements of the painting and the feelings it evoked in each of them. The nine frames at the right are from a doctoral dissertation that analyzes the colors of *The Starry Night*.

Categories Are a Perspective

Categorization is not universal like the four universal structures, but it is very popular. We organize our desktop in categories by putting files in folders. We categorize the items found in a supermarket into similar areas (produce, meats, toiletries, etc.). We spend a great deal of time teaching students to sort and categorize. Yet, we seldom make it explicit that a perspective is necessary whenever we categorize something.

Students engaged in categorizing or sorting tasks are practicing what one type of grown-up scientist gives her or his life's work to: categorizing life forms. Although the content might be different, the cognitive skill is the same. Whether it is young children sorting buttons by color or categorizing clothing into fall, winter, spring, and summer, or older students learning to categorize eukaryotes and prokaryotes, or even teachers attempting to classify student learning into Bloom's taxonomical regions, the process is the same—sorting a bunch of things into groups involves perspective taking.

The classification of biological organisms is one of our favorite human pastimes. We've invested a tremendous amount of time and effort into trying to make the diversity of life fit into groups (we also spend lots of time trying to categorize books for library systems and information for Internet systems). Where the classification of biological organisms is concerned, the general public relies on the following system: kingdom, phylum, class, order, family, genus, and species. For all intents and purposes, for the general public, that's the only way biological organisms are sorted. Yet scientists called systematists have 21 competing and valid ways to categorize organisms into species. Each of these 21 ways to categorize is based on a perspective, such as morphology (appearance). There are numerous exceptions to the rule and many types of organisms that just don't fit these schemes. For example, nearly all fungi and bacteria are generally indifferent to species boundaries. Indeed, there are so many implicit perspectives in species categorization that Allen MacNeill, a systematist, has made the radical proposition that "individual living organisms are the only things that exist in the natural world, and that species (including animal species) are quite literally figments of the human imagination."*

The point is this. When toddlers categorize picture cards or children categorize toys, or adolescents categorize baseball cards, or adults catego-

---

*MacNeill, A. The Origin of the Specious. Retrieved November 15, 2011, from http://evolutionlist.blogspot.com/2006/03/origin-of-specious.html

rize computer files, or scientists categorize findings, they all use the same skill: taking perspective.

According to Vladimiro Valerio, a cartography expert from the University of Venice, there's no such thing as a map without perspective: "Cartographers don't lie," he said, "but they take a position."* This quote appeared in a *New York Times* article featuring a globe-making outfit, "one of the biggest and best-known companies in the business," called Nova Rico. It's based in a small Italian town near the city of Florence. Nova Rico's globes land in classrooms all over the world, the United States included.

The company's directors revealed some of the fascinating distinctions they're required to make based on perspective: For Palestinians and those who live in other Arabian countries, it's commonplace to omit Israel altogether—an egregious omission, because its very existence goes unrecognized. Cyprus is divided in two for Turkish customers; but if Greeks commission the globe, it stays whole. Certain parts of Antarctica may be assigned to either Chile or Argentina, depending on who's buying. Once, the company was threatened with a boycott from Iran because a globe called the gulf between that country and Saudi Arabia the "Arabian Gulf" instead of the "Persian Gulf."**

Adopting a particular perspective can have weighty consequences. The perspectives we take, the perspectives we recognize or ignore, and those that we allow others to make for us, lie at the root of our biases and stereotypes, our worldviews and mind-sets. In our trainings across the country we have found that kids and adults alike, once we remind them of the importance of perspectives, have an easy time taking them. That is, as long as the thing that's taking the perspective has eyes (or other humanlike qualities).

Where they have significantly more trouble is taking perspectives from nonhuman or nonanimal things. For example, it's easy to take the perspective of Harry or Hillary. It is also easy to take the perspective of a hamster or a horse. That's because all of these things have "eyes" and we can easily imagine them having perspectives. But DSRP tells us that we can also take the perspective of *any* abstract idea or object. That is where some students and teachers have a more difficult time.

We have difficulty seeing that a perspective often limits the view. In other words, if we look at the entirety of music over the years, we might

*Povoledo, E. In Italy, creating worlds takes precision, yes, and politics." http://www.nytimes.com/2007/08/15/world/europe/15italy.html?ex=1344916800&en=6b2e3659850dbc10&ei=5124&partner=permalink&exprod=permalink (accessed October 27, 2008).
**Ibid.

Figure 68

see a lot of different things: styles, genres, albums sold, band names, song names, instruments used, fan culture, etc. But if we look at music solely from the perspective of hair, we see only the hair (Figure 68). All kinds of hair. Everything else other than hair fades from our view. This remarkable image is the result of taking such a perspective!

Take a look at the five perspectives in Figure 69 (hashed mirror boxes). Each perspective is on [something, anything, whatever, fill in the blank]. Notice, it's easy to take perspectives from Harry, Hillary, hamsters, or horses, but hair? How does hair have a perspective? Here are

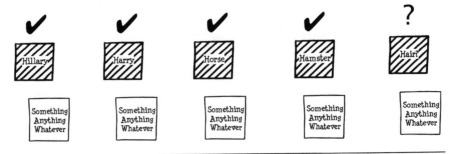

Figure 69

a few ways to practice taking perspectives from inanimate objects and abstract ideas:

1. Get a pair of large glasses and use a dry erase marker on the lenses (write the idea or object) and have your students walk around a space and point out what they see: "Put on your "texture" glasses and look at the room from the perspective of texture . . . what pops out?" They might see things like smooth, bumpy, rough, etc. This same exercise scales to things like the perspectives of rocks in geology, etc.

2. Use diagrams or tactile manipulatives and simply make every block or shape in the model into a perspective on the model itself. Using DSRP diagrams, simply add your "mirror" hash marks to every shape in the diagram and ask about the whole from each part. The poster shows just exactly how hair has a perspective. Hair sees only hair and as a result, the faces, the music, the bands, the instruments, the songs, all fade away, and we get a remarkably informative historical account of the hairstyles of popular music.

Okay, that poster in Figure 68 is cool, but can this idea of inanimate perspectives help students with their schoolwork? When Jenny, a fifth-grade student, was assigned a semester-long research project, she struggled to find a topic that would capture her attention for that long. After a week of deliberation, she decided on fashion. The teacher asked her to hone that down to something manageable. The student then said "dresses." The teacher, trying to guide the student into the assignment criteria, asked, "What about dresses can be studied in great enough depth for this big of a project?" The student replied, "Structures, and how they have changed over time to create 'fashion.'" The teacher, getting frustrated, gave the student permission to pursue the idea and hoped for the best. Jenny eagerly began her research, looking through hundreds of images in compilations from hundreds of years ago to now. In her final report, she wrote, "I looked at 60 dresses of all kinds and over 240 years from the perspective of structure." She provided the diagram in Figure 70. Jenny

Figure 70

Evolution of the Dress

Figure 71

continued: "I cut out each dress, turned them over, scanned the white side of the paper dress, and pasted it on a black background with the year the dress was made. I made a poster called 'Evolution of the Dress.'" (See Figure 71.) She then looked at them from the perspective of structure . . . but, wait, what is "structure?" Jenny asked herself, what are the parts of "structure" that I need to pay attention to in order to sort these dresses? After reading in the sources she chose for the project she focused on four: hemlines, necklines, sleeves, and waistlines. Those were the four parts of dresses that she thought of as structure. She wrote, "Dress structure can be broken into 4 parts, which can be used to analyze any dress." She provided the DSRP diagram in Figure 72, showing the 60 dresses and how she looked at them from the perspective of the four parts of structure, including necklines, sleeves, waistlines, and hemlines:

To further understand the differences over time in her dresses, Jenny needed to dig deeper (make a finer distinction among them) by identifying the parts of each one of her main structures, for example, what are the attributes of sleeves? Ideas like long, short, sleeveless, cap, bell: In total, 14 types of sleeves showed up in her research, as well as 6 different hemlines, 6 kinds of waistlines, and 12 different necklines. She wrote the

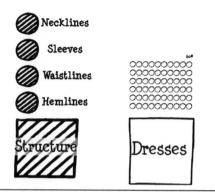

Figure 72

following followed by her diagram, "Each of these parts has parts. There are 14 types of necklines, 18 types of sleeves, and 6 types of waistlines and hemlines. I write about each of these in my report." Her DSRP diagram showed that the perspective "structure" can further be broken into four parts and that those four parts have parts. *Any* one of those parts or parts of parts can be used as a perspective on which to look at a dress (in Figure 73, all of them are hashed with the perspective hash lines).

After all her deconstructing of dress structure, Jenny thought, "How does this relate to fashion? How do designers make new and interesting dresses?" She realized that all dresses are a relationship between and among the four structures. Jenny wrote in her report, "It turns out that if you want to know what the next cool dress design will be, we can answer that question by saying: The dress is the pattern of relationships between these types of structures."

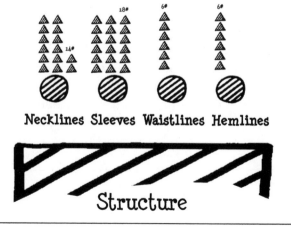

Figure 73

All dresses have the four elements, as well as the materials and crafts-manship of the dressmaker. Looking across her poster, she wondered why some dresses received more attention than others. It appeared that the dresses challenged the norm for one or more of the structures in dresses that preceded them historically. So, for example, the green slit dress worn by Jennifer Lopez at the Grammy Awards made fashion history because its construction challenged both necklines and hemlines at the same time—creating a new fashion term "the super deep V" (see Figure 74).

Classifying Dresses Using the Four Structures and Their Ranges.

Figure 74

As we saw in Figure 68—music from the perspective of hairstyles and dresses from the perspective of structure—the power of taking different perspectives on any idea lends itself not only to a deeper understanding of the topic under study but it also develops an essential thinking skill. The ability to take more than an anthropomorphic perspective—to go beyond and take a conceptual or inanimate perspective on any idea, object, or person—also opens up what and how much more you can see in general.

Ecosystems

A newly trained kindergarten teacher was eager to teach her students the elements of perspective taking. However, she was a bit apprehensive about what they could learn and how the lesson would turn out. Her class had a big unit on ecology ponds that she thought was a good venue for both introducing the elements of perspective taking and teaching them the lesson content. Her students had been studying frogs, tadpoles, and ponds for a week, and she wanted to extend their learning with DSRP.

To begin their perspective-taking exercise, Ms. Bradley had the students identify several animals that shared the pond as their home: frog, duck, turtle, fish, and tadpoles. Using the mural as the center of the students' attention, she gave each of them a picture of an animal on the list and asked the students to act like that animal, think like that animal, and answer the question, "If you were a [frog/duck/turtle, etc.], why is this pond important to you?"

The students discussed all of the things that an animal might think about a pond, like "a place to lay eggs," or "a place to sleep in the winter." To Ms. Bradley's surprise, her students wanted to explore the relationship between and among the animals when they asked "who eats whom?" and "what is food for the frog?" and "what do the lily pads eat?" To help her students sort out the answers to these questions, she focused them back on perspective-taking skills and she asked, one at a time, "From the point of view of a [frog/turtle/fish, etc.], what is food?" "What is not food?" The students soon realized that it appeared that the duck's food was not immediately obvious in the pond ecosystem and it became something they wanted to explore later.

At the same time that they gained a good understanding of pond life, and the interconnectedness of an ecosystem, Ms. Bradley's students also understood several important ideas, such as (1) a perspective is the relationship between a point (the animal) and a view (the pond); (2) we can better answer our questions when we take many perspectives; and (3) the distinction we draw about an idea (in this case, food) depends on the perspective we take (the frog/duck/turtle). In other words, what we see depends on the perspective from which we look at something.

Many More Examples of Perspective Taking

Proficiency in perspective taking is essential to creative, critical, interdisciplinary, scientific, and prosocial thinking. Perspective lies at the core of many fundamental skills like empathy and compassion. There are many opportunities to develop this skill in students with very little effort in existing curricula. Here are several examples:

- A pre-K teacher sorted buttons with her students to distinguish between the concepts of color, size, and texture to describe physical objects (Figure 75).

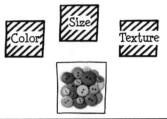

Figure 75

- A kindergarten teacher taught a standard on seasonal changes and had her students look at clothing from the perspective of seasons (Figure 76).

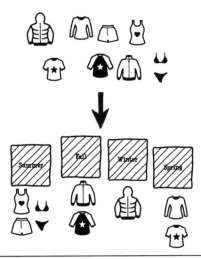

Figure 76

- An elementary art teacher had students look at nine famous paintings from the perspective of shape, color, line, genre, and feeling (Figure 77).

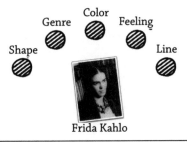

Figure 77

- A middle school geology teacher has his students understand rocks by looking at them form several perspectives: luster, hardness, color, streak, and cleavage (Figure 78).

Figure 78

- A high school language arts teacher deconstructed a novel with her students based on five perspectives: theme, suspense, character, conflict, and setting (Figure 79).

Figure 79

- An 11th-grade teacher showed students how to solve mathematical problems from two perspectives: polar and Cartesian coordinate systems (Figure 80).

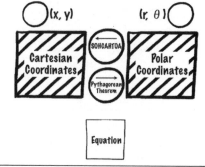

Figure 80

- A teacher resolved a dispute between students by having them take one another's perspective on the conflict and distinguish among the parts of their perspectives on the conflict (Figure 81).

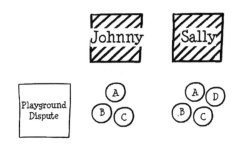

Figure 81

- A history teacher helped students to understand any war or historical event from several perspectives (Figure 82).

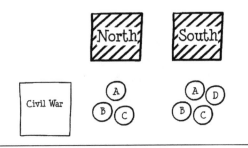

Figure 82

- A leading heart dynamicist researcher made massive scientific discoveries when he looked at physical systems from the perspective of a blood cell (Figure 83).

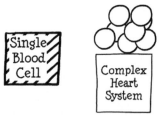

Figure 83

Like all the four universal structures, seeing both elements of perspective (both point and view) deepens understanding in any area of study and creates students who will challenge lines that are drawn for them, check their own assumptions, and be more thoughtful.

CHAPTER SIX

Conclusions and Looking Forward

Case Research: Re-Membering Information Versus Re-Building Knowledge

Imagine a 10-year-old girl named Anna who is not a star student. Because our system narrowly defines normalcy and because she has attention-deficit hyperactivity disorder (ADHD), Anna struggles with testing, homework assignments, reading, and writing. Her bouncing off the walls indoors translates into a healthy athletic intelligence outdoors. Her lack of linearity, which handicaps her writing and reading, is a strength in art and creative affairs. Her tactile intuition and penchant for patterns make her an excellent learner of big ideas, but it can cause her to lack attention for details, like what day of the week it is. Make no mistake, Anna is bright, but her test scores and grades do not reflect that. Her mind races so fast that she can't stay focused unless she is engaged. For example, she loves Legos, but Lego kits just do not engage her. Anna received an assignment to write a report on early humans. There were many requirements of the process that she had to use to create the report (notecards, using different source materials, outlining, etc.), and she also had to give an oral presentation at the end of the term. She was excited to study the topic, but the process she was required to go through was stultifying. Boring. Painful. When we interviewed her parents, we discovered that the process often "reduced her to tears."

What's happening here? Anna is a nonlinear thinker. She sees things in splats, not linear progressions. Because the process that her teachers required of her was designed for linear, linguistic types, she had great difficulty with the assignment. As a result, Anna had to think linearly in order to write her report and give a presentation. But the nature of Anna's brain means that she can't just sit down and write an outline or paper. *First she must structure the information in a way that makes sense to her and then linearize it for the purpose of writing it.* Some people think well in linear outlines, but others do not.

Good thinking leads to good writing. Anna was being asked to engage in a writing process before she had engaged in a thinking process. For a linguistic, linear learner, this would pose no particular problems because both their thinking and writing are linguistic and linear. But for a tactile, spatial, kinesthetic learner, thinking doesn't occur in neat groupings of words and outlines. It occurs as splats of prelinguistic thoughts that are related in a network.

Armed with more than 180 notecards containing facts she had gleaned from three sources, Anna sat down to write. But she was overwhelmed, struggling, and she just didn't know where to start. We introduced DSRP to Anna to help her to structure her information about early humans. We helped her to recognize six distinct groups of hominids (Australopithecus, Homo habilis, Homo erectus, Neanderthal, Homo sapiens, Cro-Magnon). There were five evolutionary perspectives (tools, diet, behavior, looks, and fossils). At the crossroads of the relationship between each distinct hominid and each evolutionary perspective was a fact or set of facts she had collected about hominid evolution. Figure 85 shows the DSRP diagram that she created.

Anna also built a tactile physical model of the diagram that she used for two purposes: (1) to linearize her nonlinear thinking into an outline to write her paper; and (2) to use as a tool during her parent presentation night, where she gave the same presentation in several ways because she could enter the conversation from any part of the model (that's one of the benefits of a nonlinear model). Her physical model was built using classroom blocks as a direct analog to the DSRP diagram. This is important because it means that you can structure information meaningfully by using DSRP in both two- and three-dimensional formats.

In video case interviews of Anna, we documented her process and her final presentation and written report. All were excellent, as confirmed by her parents and teachers, as well as the other parents she presented to. All in all, it was a good example of how DSRP structures information in order

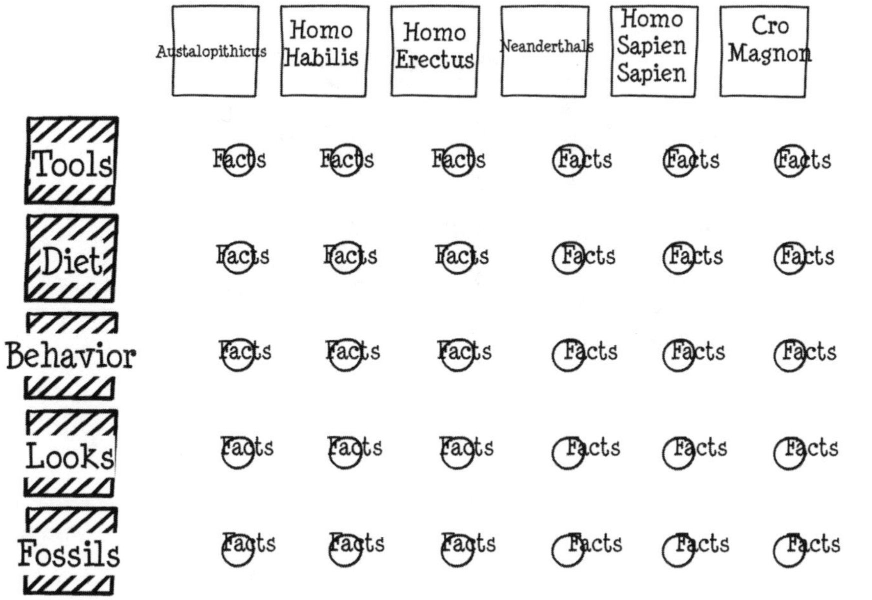

	Australopithicus	Homo Habilis	Homo Erectus	Neanderthals	Homo Sapien Sapien	Cro Magnon
Tools	Facts	Facts	Facts	Facts	Facts	Facts
Diet	Facts	Facts	Facts	Facts	Facts	Facts
Behavior	Facts	Facts	Facts	Facts	Facts	Facts
Looks	Facts	Facts	Facts	Facts	Facts	Facts
Fossils	Facts	Facts	Facts	Facts	Facts	Facts

Figure 85

to give it meaning for the student. Cool, yes? But not terribly remarkable? But wait . . . One year later, we re-interviewed Anna. We provided her with a pencil and paper if she needed it and asked her a simple, direct question with no additional prompting: "Tell us what you remember about the early hominid report you did last year."

Anna quickly directed her eyes up into her forehead as if seeing her thoughts splat.

Then she hunkered down over the paper, with her hair and arms occluding our view of what she was writing. After a few squiggles, she revealed a horizontal line of six squares and another vertical line of five squares as shown in Figure 87.

Then she began writing text onto each square, looking upward toward the mental image in her head as she wrote . . . Homo habilis . . . Cro-Magnon . . . Australopithecus. Then she filled in the text for the five evolutionary perspectives: tools used . . . how they looked . . . what they ate . . . fossil remains. Then she filled in every little fact one by one, at the cross-section of the hominid names (distinctions) and the evolutionary perspectives. When she was done, she described in great detail her entire model, flexibly. We asked her questions about the model from different "angles" or "entry points" and she would start from our questions and construct an answer that traversed the entire model. Then we

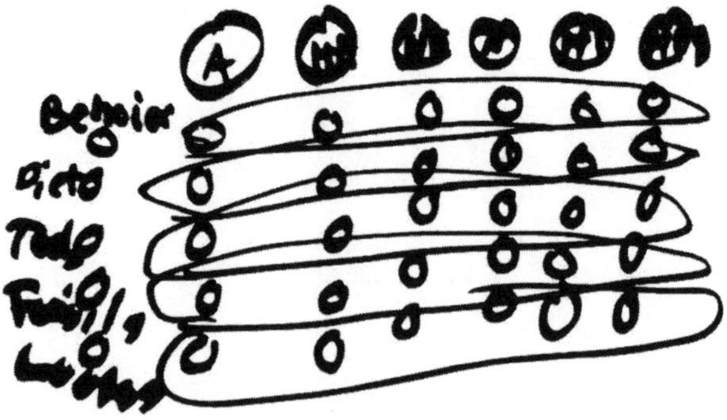

Figure 87

asked another question from a different angle, and she would start from that different question and answer as she traversed the entire model. That is knowledge-ability. Anna had been asked to recall something she had worked on over a year earlier. We know that recall decreases dramatically within one day of a test and continues to decline *each day* afterward. Most of us cannot remember things we learned in a class a year ago. *So, why was Anna able to remember so much of what she had worked on so long ago?* The answer is simple: She did not have to re-member; she re-built. This is the most important thing you should take away from Anna's case: Anna didn't recall information; she reconstructed it. This was evident the moment that she first drew the structures onto her paper and *then* added the information on early hominids.

She laid down the structures (made distinctions, formed part/whole systems, drew relationships, and took perspectives) in her drawing, long before she added the content information (Cro-Magnon, fossil remains, etc.). Researchers on expertise have learned a lot by studying how novices and experts respond differently to certain stimuli. What much of the research has found is that experts structure their information in meaningful ways whereas novices do not. For example, an expert in systematics, the study of how we classify organisms, might structure their knowledge thus: Organisms belong to different part/whole groups depending on the perspective one takes. Whereby, from the perspective of shared physical characteristics, species might be organized according to the traditional Linnaean system of biological classification: kingdom, phylum, class, order, family, genus, and species. Alternatively, from a cladistic perspective (evolutionary relationships) the organisms would group differently. There are 21 different scientifically valid perspectives from which we can

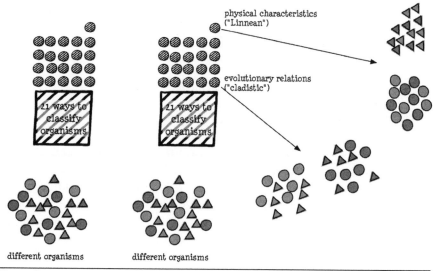

different organisms   different organisms

Figure 88

choose, depending on the characteristics we highlight. The DSRP diagram for these perspectives is shown in Figure 88. A novice understands biological classification in the following way: "Using the pneumonic device 'Kings Play Chess On Fridays Generally Speaking' I can recall the way organisms are grouped into a hierarchy of kingdom, phylum, class, order, family, genus, species."

Notice that the novice view structures the information as well, but the structure is meaningless, because a pneumonic device will remember the information but not reconstruct it. In other words, there is nothing meaningful about the relationship between "play" in the device and "phylum" other than that they both start with the letter "p." Of course, any structuring, no matter how low-fidelity or meaningless, can be modeled with DSRP because it is universal to all ideas—even bad ones. So we can diagram the novice's understanding below where the primary perspective is "this is how I remember how to classify things" and the relationships are between the shared letters of the pneumonic device and the classification system (see Figure 89). Also notice that the expert's knowledge structure is highly adaptable, as was Anna's, whereas the novice's knowledge structure is static. Very little about it can change and still function adequately. The expert's structure is capable of adapting to another 100 years of innovation in the science of classification without significant problems.

Although the sophistication level of experts' structures differs from those of novices, both novices and experts often share a lack of conscious

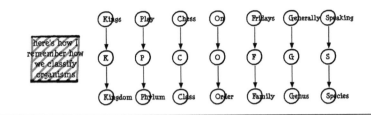

Figure 89

awareness of the structures that they are using. This explains why, for example, so many brilliant experts are such terrible teachers. It's because they know what they know, but they don't know how they know it and therefore they cannot help the students construct an understanding of the new knowledge. In Anna's case, she not only can reconstruct the content, but she also has a language for making the underlying structures explicit and a set of tools such as diagrams and tactile manipulatives. Anna understood her knowledge structures *explicitly,* which has profound implications for her prospects as a lifelong learner.

Because Anna is conscious of her knowledge structures and uses them explicitly to build knowledge, she not only knows stuff, but she knows how she knows stuff. As a result, she would be a great teacher. Being a lifelong learner, in a nutshell, means being your own best teacher. So, if Anna has co-located both the role of learner and teacher in the same little body, then she's well on her way to being a lifelong learner.

One can begin to see that there is more to Anna's use of DSRP than meets the eye. There's a lot going on "under the hood," so to speak. She's not only moving toward something that looks a lot like expertise, she's developing what is called "deep understanding" rather than *Jeopardy*-like recall. This deep understanding is not only of the content she is required to or interested in learning but also of her own knowledge-building processes, which lead to her being an excellent teacher and eventually a lifelong autodidactic learner. That's a lot to pack into a little report on early hominids. But wait . . . there was an unexpected twist in Anna's case.

Case Research: From Hominids to Egyptians?

A year later, two years after her early hominids report, Anna had another report to do about ancient Egyptians. This time she had a head start: There were no tears, just hard work and enthusiasm. Anna used the process she had been taught by using DSRP and immediately came up with a good

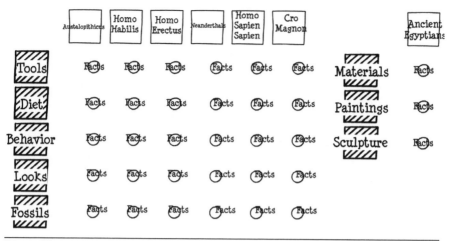

	Australopithicus	Homo Habilis	Homo Erectus	Neanderthals	Homo Sapien Sapien	Cro Magnon			Ancient Egyptians
Tools	Facts	Facts	Facts	Facts	Facts	Facts	Materials		Facts
Diet	Facts	Facts	Facts	Facts	Facts	Facts	Paintings		Facts
Behavior	Facts	Facts	Facts	Facts	Facts	Facts	Sculpture		Facts
Looks	Facts	Facts	Facts	Facts	Facts	Facts			
Fossils	Facts	Facts	Facts	Facts	Facts	Facts			

Figure 90

structure for her understanding of ancient Egyptians—one that she would eventually linearize into a written report. Then she had a eureka! moment, as she looked at her new diagram on Egyptians. Something looked familiar. Wait . . . it was a lot like her diagram about early hominids! She was so excited.

Here's what Anna saw, side by side, with her early hominids and ancient Egyptian reports (see Figure 90). What you witnessed was "transfer," the Holy Grail of education and learning. Transfer is precious. If we can teach our students to be efficient transferrers of knowledge, then whenever they learn one thing, they can teach themselves 10, 20, 50, 100, or 1,000 things. They can apply that knowledge in many other domains and situations. We get more for less. They can take something that wasn't meant to solve a particular problem in a particular domain and use it to solve that problem anyway. That's what we typically think of as brilliant, inventive, creative, innovative, or genius behavior.

Anna's knowledge of *how* she knows and what she knows is very adaptable because of the DSRP structures. Anna saw that the structure of one project could transfer to another project and as a result she didn't need to reinvent the wheel. In addition, she discovered that the same structure is a pretty good template (what we call a common structure) for lots of other similar types of reports.

Deep understanding and transfer are, for all intents and purposes, the most remarkable of all the outcomes of learning. But these two outcomes do not receive the attention they deserve in our existing educational systems. They are the two things we see most as outcomes of DSRP.

DSRP Blocks of Knowledge

One evening while Laura made dinner, her 6-year-old daughter, Gianna, who had been doing her homework, appeared next to her with 10 little pieces of paper in her hand. The pieces were her spelling list: Each scrap contained one word she was supposed to learn to spell. "Why did you do that to your spelling list?" Laura asked her. Gianna shrugged: "So I can do stuff with it." Gianna found that grasping abstract concepts, such as words, was much easier if she could turn them into physical objects—in this case, into pieces of paper that she could hold, feel, and manipulate. Gianna is not alone. Although some students easily absorb abstract knowledge directly, many do not, and everybody can benefit from integrating the sense of touch into the learning process.

Research in education and cognitive science has shown that humans are "knowledge architects." We build knowledge through thinking and through our interaction with information. As Gianna's story illustrates, the connection between tactile activity and conceptual construction is deeply instinctual. The modern field of haptics—the study of how humans use touch and kinesthetics to acquire information—has established that touch and movement are deeply connected with the process of constructing knowledge. Other findings reveal how movement, gesture, and vision play a role in the process of constructing knowledge. For example, a baby's exploration of the world through touch begins as early as a few months of age and continues in various ways throughout childhood.*

Jean Piaget, the noted child psychologist, demonstrated that the use of the sense of touch through object manipulation increased children's ability to create mental constructs of the world (build knowledge) in different age groups.** One of Piaget's students, the MIT professor Seymour Papert, proposed not only that children build knowledge but also that they need to construct it, literally, in physical forms or models. He emphasized that people learn most easily when they physically put things together, as with Legos or blocks. He concluded that better learning did not come from finding "better ways for the teacher to instruct, but from giving the learner better opportunities to construct."***

Laboratory and field studies have shown that integrating tactile activities into the classroom improves students' learning by bringing multiple sensory systems and areas of the brain into the learning process,

---

*Kuhn, E. "Google Unveils Top Political Searches of 2009." CNN, http://politicalticker.blogs.cnn.com/2009/12/18/google-unveils-top-political-searches-of-2009/ (accessed August 2011).
**Piaget, J. *The construction of reality in the child.* New York: Basic Books, 1954.
***Papert, S. *The connected family.* Atlanta: Longstreet Press, 1996.

improving retention and developing and reinforcing core thinking skills. Much research into haptic learning has established connections among touch, kinesthetics, activity, and improved learning.*Learning through the haptic system is stronger than visual learning alone. This calls for attention to touch as an integral and important part of children's learning.

The connection between the hand and the mind already manifests in a myriad of tactile manipulatives seen in classrooms all over the world. Manipulative play in classrooms draws on haptics to make the crucial hand-mind connection, using the students' inherent multimodal tendency to relate movement to mental activity. Teachers have used manipulatives—wooden blocks, math beads, sandpaper letters, coins—for as long as schools have existed, across many generations. Gianna created her own when she turned one long list of spelling words into moveable, touchable strips of paper. This act was purposeful, and she instinctively knew that she needed to do it to memorize, to be able to handle, that daunting list of words. Touch, as an integral part of thinking (and, thus, learning), provides students with concrete experiences with intangible concepts and ideas.

Using blocks or other common toys (such as Russian matryoshka nesting dolls) can be powerful tools to develop thinking skills and encourage people to play with ideas. An analysis of 75 studies on the importance of block play showed that block play contributes to cognitive development, and the study confirmed, "the benefits of [block] play have been well supported by the theories and research of the past century." This holds true today, as a recent American Academy of Pediatrics study concluded: "Play is important to healthy brain development." Through play, children use their creativity to develop "imagination, dexterity, and physical, cognitive, and emotional strength."

The construction paradigm reminds us that our hands are integrated with our brains. As such, doing, playing, and manipulating with the hands is an essential part of learning and thinking. Children actively build knowledge in a similar way to how they might construct a toy bridge out of toothpicks or erect a crane out of various parts. In his autobiography, Frank Lloyd Wright spoke about the influence of toy building blocks on his early development. Generations of children learned about the built world, geometry, mathematics, architecture, design, and creativity from such classic toys as Lincoln Logs, Legos, Tinker Toys, and Erector Sets. These construction sets introduced us to the built world. In the same way

---

*Minogue, J. & Jones, M. G. (2006). "Haptics in education: Exploring an untapped sensory modality." *Review of Educational Research, 76* (3), 317–348.

that children of the industrial age had toys to build physical structures, building knowledge requires a unique construction kit that allows children (and adults) to model, see, and manipulate ideas in their hands, which also develops important thinking skills. Taking a "constructive" approach to knowledge, where children are encouraged to build ideas visually and/or tactically—in a similar way that they might draw or build a bridge or a skyscraper—will go a long way in developing the kinds of thinkers we need; thinkers who will thrive in the knowledge age.

Applying DSRP to 21st-Century Education

While knowledge and thinking skills have always been important, globalization makes them more critical now than ever before. Globalization creates more and more links, interconnecting people and places that used to seem separate and unrelated. Problems are no longer contained in their own geographical areas but are linked to and impact other problems across the globe.

We don't know about you, but we never used to worry about how chickens are handled in China. But we do now. You probably do, too, because a strain of avian flu that was similar to the one we see today had killed 5% of the global population in 1918. That virus is now only 17 hours away from us by plane. Even though Asia hasn't moved any closer to us, it is more interconnected with us. Its problems are our problems.

Our problems in the United States have moved closer to Asia, too. In 2003, one single cow in Washington State caught "Mad Cow Disease." In less than a minute, the news of this poor unsuspecting cow's malady traveled—via the Internet—across oceans and continents to South Korea. As soon as South Korea caught wind of the problem on the Web, it banned all American beef imports, costing the U.S. beef industry $850 million. In this interconnected age, even the tiniest things can wreak global havoc.

When Larry Page and Sergey Brin, two Stanford graduate students, founded Google in 1997, only a gaggle of geeks were googling. They searched for geeky things. Ten years later, in November 2007, the number of people googling had exponentially increased to 112 million. What was the number one search term that month? iPhone. A gaggle of geeks googling grew in one decade to 112 million people searching for what?—a device that allows them to google anywhere, anytime. Today, Google processes more than one billion search requests every day.*

---

*http://understandingbignumbers.com/google-searches.each-day

From either-or to and-both thinking: Research conducted with college students from both Kyoto, Japan, and from Michigan has demonstrated the significant differences between Eastern and Western styles of thought. Students were shown videos depicting an underwater scene that contained fast and slow fish, water, bubbles, plant life, rocks, and so on. Japanese and American students described the scene differently. While both mentioned the fish (the "identity") equally, Japanese students also mentioned background components (the "other") 60% more often than the Americans. Japanese students also mentioned the hidden relationships with surrounding objects ("the fish wove through the grasses") twice as often. The study also noted that Japanese students spoke first of the environment ("it's a scene in a pond"), while American students first mentioned the fish.

The study concluded that "Asians see the big picture and they see objects in relation to their environments—so much so that it can be difficult for them to visually separate objects from their environments. Westerners focus on objects while slighting the field and they literally see fewer objects and relationships in the environment than do Asians."*

It's tempting to conclude that one thought style is better than the other but the truth is that the 21st century calls for both types of thinking: We have to zoom in and to zoom out, to split and to lump, to take various perspectives. In short, the 21st-century thinker needs to hold two opposed ideas in the mind at the same time and still retain the ability to function.

Our legal system (guilty, not guilty), technology, (1s and 0s), and worldview (us, them) to name a few, are all based on bivalency—the either-or logic of Aristotle (true, false). When we consider the 21st-century thinking skills we need in order to navigate effectively within our increasingly interconnected planet, it behooves us to expand our vision in both the macro and the micro. It's the power of multivalency or and-both. The power of the DSRP Method is the power of and-both. The four universal structures allow us to create definitive boundaries in one moment and challenge those boundaries in the next. In the end, we hold both in full view. The implications of this multivalent or "and-both" thinking cannot be underestimated—with "and-both," we can create mental models that are more accurate to the real world. In short, mental models that are out of alignment with the real world are useless. Mental models that are aligned with the real world can be used to navigate and change it.

---

*Rochat, P. et al. (2003). The role of modeling and request type on symbolic comprehension of objects and gestures in young children. *Journal of Child Language, 30,* 27–45.

At its core, globalization is about adding more links between things. The world gets more and more interconnected one link at a time. But links are like rabbits—they breed and multiply. Hyperlinks beget more hyperlinks, friendships beget more friendships, customers beget more customers, and treaties beget more treaties.

We often tell our students that cause and effect are not neighbors on a timeline. Because the world is so interconnected, this is more true today than ever before. Many things that you wouldn't think are connected will turn out to be interrelated in this new world. Strange things correlate. What's the connection between Montana wheat, Louisiana shrimp, and Saudi oil? In an effort to solve the decrease in crop yields caused by pests, we innovated a solution: pesticides. These pesticides led to the leeching of nitrates into soil, which then traveled via the thousands of streams and tributaries in the Mississippi River Basin and emptied into the Gulf of Mexico. Here, pesticides, which once were a solution to a problem, created an even bigger problem. Nitrates created algae blooms that depleted oxygen levels in the Gulf of Mexico, decimating all life in an area the size of Delaware and Connecticut combined. We now call this area where the Mississippi empties into the gulf the "dead zone," because a place that once provided some of the best shrimping and crabbing in the world is now barren of all life. . . . Meanwhile, the price of a barrel of oil has increased dramatically because of many factors, including the war in Iraq, and many shrimp boat captains can't afford the fuel that they need to get out to the area where the crabs and shrimp still inhabit the waters. Those still in business, naturally, incorporate the price of the fuel into the price of their catch, and your shrimp cocktail just got more expensive. The more things are interconnected, the more often we see the unintended consequences that turn ingenious solutions into deleterious problems.

These ever-multiplying links make the whole world increasingly interconnected, and as a result, problems are becoming intractable, durable, hearty, complex, and tougher to solve. There was a time when "loners in labs" could solve these problems, but modern problems require more knowledge and expertise than any single person can gain in a lifetime. The solutions we need in the 21st century require interdisciplinary "teams at tables." The intractable problems we face—global warming, world health crises, terrorism, even globalization itself—pay no attention to disciplinary boundaries; they cut across social, political, scientific, theological, and financial domains. This will only be more true as we move further into the 21st century. We can't even begin to guess what the coming problems of this century will be. To meet the challenges ahead, problem solvers in this new age need integrative proficiency in the following ways of thinking:

- **Content knowledge:** They need to know something about an area or field of study.
- **Critical thinking:** They need to be analytical and logical in framing problems.
- **Creative thinking:** They'll need to think differently to address these tough, interconnected problems.
- **Interdisciplinary thinking:** Problems don't respect disciplinary boundaries, and neither will the needed solutions.
- **Scientific thinking:** They must have a capacity to question, analyze, and use information to address problems in a formal way.
- **Systems thinking:** They must understand the interconnectedness of systems, concentric circles of context, and unintended consequences.
- **Prosocial thinking (emotional intelligence):** Because they're working with a team at a table, they'll need to be able to talk, listen, and collaborate with others to resolve problems.

As an educator, it is your job to train the problem solvers of the future. It is your job to stock these "teams at tables" with graduates who possess 21st-century skills so that they can solve the world's most pressing problems and contribute to society. Teaching 21st-century skills means teaching students not only what to know (content knowledge), but also how to know (thinking skills).

In 1900, 8 out of 10 jobs involved working with one's hands. In 2000, the statistic flipped—8 out of 10 jobs involved working with ideas.[3] Where schools once needed students to master the laws of the physical world to navigate an industrial age, today we live in the knowledge age. So what do we need to understand today? This is not a trick question. The answer is the laws of knowledge. Like the laws of physics, the laws of knowledge are simple. But be warned, just like Newton's Laws, what seems simple on its surface can be sublime. Do not let its simplicity disguise the universally important implications of the equation for knowledge:

$$K = I \times T\{DSRP\}$$

This is a simple equation but it has deep roots in scientific research, a long history in scholarly discourse, and complex names in academic terminology. It's brief, instantly comprehensible, and it holds the potential to transform how educators work.

In our professional development trainings around the country and the world, we are often asked by teachers, "Why does the DSRP Method work so well in my classroom?" The reason they ask is that the results they see in the classroom seem to go well beyond simply teaching thinking skills. Teachers see increased student engagement. They see their students going beyond memorizing facts to a deep understanding of topical content. They see test scores increase. They see their own effectiveness and engagement as teachers increase. Many have told us that the DSRP Method has reignited that intangible love of learning and teaching that initially drew them to want to be teachers. They want to know why these impacts are occurring just from using a method. We explain it in this way. When teachers use the DSRP Method, their energy is focused on the two most effective relationships in education today. They are (1) the student-teacher relationship and (2) the knowledge-thinking relationship (see Figure 92).

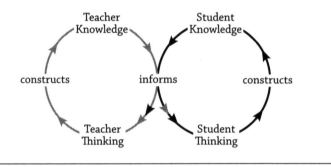

Figure 92

When we focus on these two relationships, the ripple effect is that we get many best practices for free without explicitly trying to get them. For example, you'll see one or more of the following practices in classrooms everywhere:

- Differentiated instruction
- Student-centered learning
- Multiple intelligences
- Teacher effectiveness
- Data-driven assessment
- Deep understanding
- 21st-century skills
- Critical thinking
- Creative thinking

- Interdisciplinary thinking
- Systems thinking
- Scientific thinking
- Prosocial thinking
- Cooperative learning
- Experiential learning
- Project-based learning
- Understanding by design
- Rigor and relevance
- Brain-based education
- Integrated curricula
- Character education
- Assessment and grading
- Standards-based learning
- Mind mapping and graphic organizers
- Executive function
- Nonlinguistic representation
- Note taking and summarizing

All of these effects are the natural output of zeroing in on these two relationships.

We've already discussed the knowledge-thinking relationship. It is an inseparable and dynamic cycle. When we think, we build more knowledge. We become more knowledgeable. At the same time, this knowledge helps us to think even better. It's a positively reinforcing loop with exponential payoffs. Equally important is that by focusing on the thinking and knowledge creation of the child, we are building the relationship between teachers and students. It is this relationship that acts as the central conduit for learning. But why would this lead to such remarkable benefits and best practices?

René Descartes, the father of modern Western science, said, "I think, therefore I am." Buddha, the father of Eastern philosophy, said, "We are what we think. With our thoughts we create the world." What both of these sayings reveal is the absolutely essential role that thinking plays in shaping our identity. This holds true for our students. A teacher who is keyed in to what and how their students are thinking will see their students for who they are. As a result, students feel recognized when their thoughts are acknowledged and valued by their teacher. This increases not only competence in any subject matter, but also the students' confidence when approaching new knowledge. When students are encouraged to think about their own thinking, they learn about themselves.

If the relationship between a teacher and student is focused on knowledge and thinking, then the focal point of learning is on the students' construction in relation to the goal of the knowledge being learned (a fact, the Civil War, Pythagorean theorem, seasonal change, whatever). If the teacher and student have a method to recognize and communicate the construction of an idea, then they can do three things of great importance. First, they can see the (intended) construction of the idea that is the goal of learning (say, seasonal change). Second, they can see the student's construction of the idea. And third, they can compare and contrast the two in order to assess where thinking must be directed or corrected. For example, researchers at Harvard University found that in order to understand seasonal change, students must identify 11 ideas and relate them in a systematic way.* This research found that 21 of the 23 graduates, alumni, and faculty interviewed could not properly identify, relate, and systematize these 11 concepts to answer the question "Why do we have seasons?" Their knowledge of seasonal change was different from the valid knowledge of seasonal change—it was mismatched. Identifying the mismatch between the goal ideas (the test, etc.) and the students' construction of the ideas is universally important in education and holds true for any topic or idea in any grade from pre-K to PhD. We can call this type of comparison "construct matching," because we map the student's thinking on to the factual knowledge that will be on the test.

Education today is complex, and it's easy to get caught up in the hubbub of the administrivia, the newest technological gizmo, the debates on classroom size or this or that theory, budgets, and behavioral problems. The DSRP Method cuts through all the noise and helps us to find the signal. When we use the DSRP Method in the classroom, the focus of education is where it should be—on the students' constructions of the world and on teacher effectiveness in helping children to build knowledge. Most importantly, they will be able to think . . . and they will thrive.

---

*Schneps, M. (1989). Private universe project. Harvard University.

Common Structures
Old and New Insights in Metacognition

The Power of Analogies for 21st-Century Thinking

Can you remember what research was like *before* the Internet? We used to look things up in books! Can you remember how messages were sent *before* email? Do you remember sending, and receiving, hand-written letters via the U.S. Postal Service? The Internet, as we know it today, began in 1989 with the invention of the web browser. For most of the population, email service wasn't common until 1993. Since then, a lot has changed. Sometimes, it's hard to comprehend that our students weren't alive before the Internet or email. Fewer still understand the cultural significance of *Star Wars*. But we share a common bond with our students. We can't understand what life was like in the 14th century, *before* the invention of analogies.

That statement sounds absurd. Was there a time before analogies? Haven't there always been analogies? Aren't analogies like rocks ... they've been around forever, right? It turns out that analogies are no different than iPhones. Analogies are a form of technology—a conceptual tool that was *invented* to increase our ability to communicate and to understand. In the Medieval Ages, before analogies existed, there were a number of problems associated with the use of words that had more than one sense. Logicians (people who studied logic), theologians (people who studied God), and metaphysicists were concerned about the confusing nature of existence. For example, how the word "animal" could be used to describe actual animals or representations of animals (i.e., the same word, different referents). It was a big problem and it required a solution. The solution, the great technological breakthrough, was the analogy (Figure 93).

Figure 93

Here are three paradigm-shifting technological innovations and their numbers of users:

- iPhone users: 44,000
- Facebook users: 500,000
- Analogy users: 7,046,548,000

The 14th century marked the beginning of the Renaissance, which created an intellectual transformation. So, in many ways, the popularization of analogies was a sign of the times, like Facebook is a sign of a new social transformation, the age of Web 2.0 in which everyone is connected.

Stop. Did you notice anything? We just made an analogy but we suspect that your brain processed it like your stomach digests chicken soup—easy. (Oops, there's another one.) We can hardly refrain from using analogies because they are, like oxygen, pervasive. Because analogies are so common we barely notice them. Here's the analogy made above in a visual form (see Figure 94).

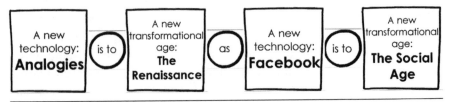

Figure 94

It's hard enough to remember what it was like before Facebook, and harder still to remember back in time before email and the Internet. Remembering a time before the automobile is beyond most of us, but we can imagine it or recall a movie scene with cobblestone streets and horse-drawn carriages. But remembering what the world was like before we had analogies seems incomprehensible. We can't even imagine this world with the help of a movie set or an old daguerreotype photograph.

Analogy Technology

There are a few things about analogies that make them advanced technology:

- *Analogies are "common structures"*: The cornerstone of analogy technology is that it is a common conceptual structure. That is, it's a concept that is so common that all of us do it. Not every concept or idea we have is an analogy but every person makes analogies. We do it a lot. The genius behind the invention of analogies was that they gave us a mental model of a common mental model.

- *Analogies are content agnostic*: The common structure we call an analogy is content agnostic because the structure of an analogy stays the same even though the content might be different. Take, for example, the two analogies in Figure 95.

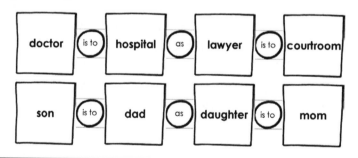

Figure 95

- *The underlying structure of the analogy is universally common*: Notice that in both analogies in the figure, the structure of each (the shapes and their spatial relationships) is the same even though the content of each (the words) is different. Of course, analogies are only partially content agnostic because the content of the relationships remains the same for all analogies (namely, X *is to* Y *as/like* P *is to* Q). We will see other common structures later on that are totally content agnostic.

Analogies are *very* common, but they are not universal. In other words, not every thought we have is an analogy but a lot of the thoughts we have are analogies. What makes something common versus universal? When something is universal, it is omnipresent—it is present always, anywhere, anytime. Analogies are not in every single thought we have so they are not always present. This doesn't make analogies any less important. Douglas Hofstadter, a Distinguished Professor of Cognitive Science at Indiana University in Bloomington, said, "Analogy is the core of cognition." If he means that analogies are absolutely critical to cognition (thinking), then he's right. But if we take him literally by using the dictionary definition of "core," "the central or most important part of something," then Hofstadter's statement overreaches. How can we tell? When something is universal, then it is omnipresent in everything. When something is universal it is a basic ingredient of everything. So, we can either look for things that don't contain analogies or in which an analogy is not necessary, or we can look at the structure of an analogy and identify more basic elements that make it up.

In the case of analogies, we can see that they are made up of smaller elements that are revealed by the DSRP Method. Let's take a deeper look at the structure of an analogy from the perspective of the DSRP Method:

- *Distinctions*: Each of the structural objects in a diagram is a distinction. DSRP makes explicit even more distinct identities than are revealed in the analogical structures.

- *Relationships*: One of the things that traditional analogical notation and structure reveals best is the relational nature of an analogy. But, even with these relationships revealed, much remains hidden.

- *Systems*: An analogy is actually one system (rectangle) made up of two parts (ovals) and a relationship (middle triangle). In turn, each of these ovals is a whole made up of a "barbell" set of parts. Using DSRP diagrams, we can reconstruct traditional analogical notation to see these additional structures very easily.

- *Perspectives*: Each of the structural objects in this analogy is also a perspective. For example, the middle relationship (triangle) does not interact with the inner triangle-parts but with the ovals to form a *simile*. A simile is a structure in which to things are *like* each other (the world is like a stage) whereas a metaphor is a structure in which two things *are* each other (the world is a stage). If we view the analogy as a network of interconnected nodes, the middle relationship is actually connected to two oval systems, not to the innermost triangles within them as suggested by traditional analogical structure (Figure 96).

Figure 96

Reconstructing a traditional analogical description in this way reveals many more elements and dynamics than meets the eye. It also reveals that DSRP structures are universal to analogies, which by definition means that analogies are not core, basic, elemental, fundamental, or universal. Analogies are actually complex structures, far from the most elemental and universal structures of thought. It is no wonder that it took over 14 centuries to discover them. This by no means undermines the brilliance of the analogy technology nor does it diminish the massive importance that analogies play in everyday cognition. Simply put, analogies are one of the most remarkable common cognitive structures ever invented in the history of mankind.

The Category Cul-de-Sac

Analogies are sublime. They feel like good friends or lovers, so we can forgive them their lack of universality—even lament it. But another common structure with a similarly long history and claims to false universality has become much more insidious than our beloved analogies. That common structure is the *category*.

We could say all the same nice things about the marvelous invention of the category that we did about that of analogies. The invention of the category dates back to Aristotle (384–322 BC). Today, we can hardly imagine what it would be like to exist in a world unstructured by categorization. Like the invention of analogies, the invention of categories has given us much to admire. It is common parlance in the field of cognitive science that categories are universal cognitive structures—that we cannot survive nor have a thought without them. Yet, despite our love affair with categories, they do have a dark side. Categories are a cognitive cul-de-sac. *Cul-de-sac* is a French word that literally means "bottom of bag" and refers to a dead end in the road. This is the insidious nature of categorization: It makes us feel like we are getting somewhere—speeding down the highway of understanding and knowledge until, wham! Dead end. We're stuck. And it usually takes a long time to get unstuck.

Categories make us feel like we understand the universe because we are able to cognitively control it. The question is, does categorical structure adequately represent the real structure of the universe? Does using categories help us feel more knowledgeable or does it actually make us more knowledgeable? Let's take a look at a few examples.

- *Scientific disciplines*: The categorization of knowledge into scientific disciplines did a lot to get us "out of the gates" and "down the road" but today it is posing real problems for us. This is because the universe we are trying to understand and the problems we are trying to solve do not heed our disciplinary boundaries. The universe, and all of the problems in it, is interdisciplinary (inter-real?). University policies and financial structures, departmental culture and tenure structure, and our own thinking is hindered by the categories we set up. Our categorization of knowledge into disciplines seems to have done a lot for us but now it's turned into a cul-de-sac, which is going to take a long time to get out of.

- *Hierarchy of biological classifications*: We teach it in schools as if it is a fact but the "species concept" is wildly complex and nothing like the streamlined categories we all learned in grade school. Today, scientists have not 1 but 21 equally valid and useful perspectives on how to group organisms into species, including morphologically, ecologically, genetically, and by mate recognition. Which perspective the scientist uses depends on the job at hand. Bacteria pose significant problems for categorization. What used to be a biological freeway to understanding has become a categorical cul-de-sac.

- *Bloom's taxonomy*: Very few theories are as popular or influential in education today than Bloom's. Yet few teachers can reduce it to practice and research validates none of it. Despite this, it was recently revised, demonstrating our allegiance to categories despite their lack of fidelity. Knowledge and higher-order thinking skills are far too robust and complex to stuff into Bloom's discrete categorical prison. It's going to take years to retrain teachers to get out of this cul-de-sac.

- *Organization of the Internet, your desktop, office filing systems, libraries*: Filing systems, computer desktops and even the Internet have been organized by using categories from their origins. That's exactly why no one can find anything. It is another categorical cul-de-sac.

There are countless more examples. Worst among them are the categorization skills we are teaching to children, which lead them to be less robust and more black-and-white, less adaptive thinkers. Categories are *insidious* because it is a fitting description of how they behave: They "proceed in a gradual, subtle way, but with harmful effects." The harmful effects of the categorization cul-de-sac can be remedied with another common structure derived from DSRP theory.

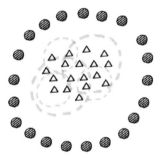
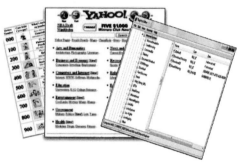

It is estimated that there are up to 100 million species. If you drew one triangle every second to represent a single species it would take you 3.17 years to finish. To organize this massive collection scientists tried categorization but it failed. Instead, they group organisms into species according to 21 scientifically valid perspectives. How do scientists know which perspective to use? It depends on what they are trying to do. Part-whole groupings based on perspectives are universal. Categorization is not.

When the web was first organized, it was categorized using vast directories like the folders on your desktop or books in a library. Searching seldom resulted in finding. Google revolutionized the web by thinking about it in relationships and perspective-groupings rather than discrete categories.

Figure 97

What DSRP structures reveal is that the application of discrete categories to real-world phenomena is never adequate. Grouping something in a single discrete way is rarely enough (see Figure 97). In addition, all categorization schema are based on a perspective (usually implicit). If we are to escape the cul-de-sac of categories but still benefit from their use today, we should replace our category schema with a part/whole-grouping-by-perspective schema.

Common Structures
DSRP Reveals Eleven New Common Structures

New Common Structures

With the remarkable impact of such common structures as analogy and category, one wonders why there haven't been more? DSRP theory has already revealed many more common structures and there is the promise of dozens or hundreds more. We will review a brief list of some of these common structures. Some will seem familiar because they are already in use, but like analogies and categories, when we are conscious of these common structures, they become even more powerful as they open up new avenues of understanding and communication. The first four common structures are D, S, R, and P themselves, which are both universal and common. The next seven structures are not universal, but are common and have emerged from DSRP.

- *Barbell:* A "barbell" gets its name for obvious reasons. The basic structure looks like a weightlifting barbell. The structure is made up of two identities and a relationship (all of which could also be wholes with parts, distinctions, or perspectives) (Figure 98).

Figure 98

- *Perspective Circle:* A perspective circle is a remarkable common structure, the utility of which is ubiquitous. Whenever we explore an idea, we can take multiple perspectives on it. As you can see in the first diagram, you can think of the object A in simple terms and look at it from four perspectives or in the second diagram it is shown that object A actually has a different part/whole structure depending on which perspective you are viewing it from. In other words, A is not always A when you take different perspectives. Notice that this common structure, like all of them, can be extrapolated to include more Ds, Ss, Rs, and Ps (Figure 99).

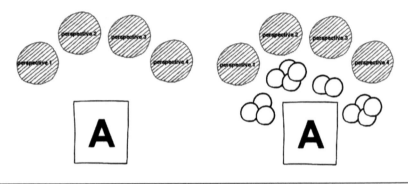

Figure 99

- *R-to-D-to-S (aka an algorithm for innovation):* It is often said that there are three ways to innovate: (1) invent something totally new, (2) make an existing product better, or (3) combine two existing things into something new. The R-to-D-to-S common structure or "algorithm for innovation" hits on all three but especially the third. It's a common process structure: (1) two things exist, (2) relate the two things (note the relationship is implicit), (3) distinguish the relationship by giving it an identity/name, (4) transform the relationship into a whole made up of

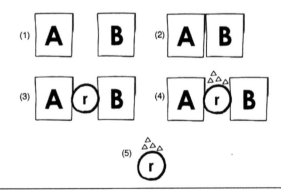

Figure 100

parts, and (5) allow the relationship to stand on its own. This algorithm for innovation is behind gas-station/minimarts and new interdisciplinary disciplines such as biochemistry (Figure 100).

- *Massively Parallel Perspectives*: Another powerful common structure yields tremendous insight into what might be called "the ecology of ideas." When we create an idea, we mustn't think of it as a discrete thing but as a system of several of many ideas as we think of the salient Ds , Ss, Rs, and Ps. Every idea is really a network of sorts rather than a single object. But while the network of our thought is expansive, it is not infinite, it has some boundary that we can call the conceptual space. This space includes a certain number of interconnected ideas— a configuration of the most salient DSRPs. We can often expand our deep understanding or alternatively assess our understanding of this space by using the massively parallel perspectives common structure. Let me give you a simple example from a lesson plan on story telling. Sixth-grade language arts students went through four steps: (1) They developed rich constructs of a story by reading several stories and breaking the stories down into parts, (2) broke down those parts into parts (e.g., time), (3) showed how their deep understanding of the parts of a story influenced their own writing as they created a story of their own that included all of the parts they diagrammed, and (4) used massively parallel perspective taking to assess whether they accomplished the task (look at their story from the perspective of each of the parts and parts of parts). The rich construct that students built in Step 1 became a checklist for self-assessment. For example, "How does my story look from the perspective of a round character?" Notice that in (4) all of the parts and parts of parts are considered as perspectives. This is an example of massively parallel perspective taking—a powerful tool for seeing the ecology of ideas and especially germane when building frameworks, theories, or other discrete mental models that must have internal consistency and validity. (See Figure 101.)

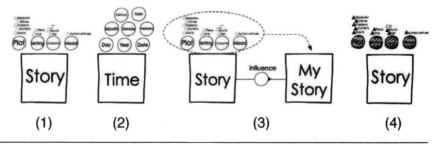

(1)   (2)   (3)   (4)

Figure 101

- *Recognizing Rs for N*: Any time you are thinking of or hear an idea that is described has having *n* number of parts, use the formula $n(n - 1)$ to determine how many relationships might need to be considered. The number of possible relationships expands quickly but this common structure helps you think things through, assist others' with their ideas, find holes or opportunities in things (critical thinking or creative thinking), and generally appear smart.

- *Part/Whole Combinatorics*: You can make many sets out of a small number of elements. Take the example below where three elements yield seven possible part/whole sets. Like the recognizing Rs for N common structure, you'll be able to quickly penetrate new ideas and proposals, think through your own thinking more clearly, or find holes or opportunities in things. Here's how many part/whole subsets there are for *n* (1–6): $n = 2, 3$; $n = 3, 7$; $n = 4, 15$; $n = 5, 31$; $n = 6, 63$. (See Figure 102.)

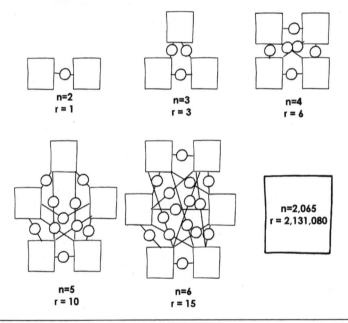

Figure 102

- *Problem-Solution Flip*: Why are the clouds so pink in a sunrise? It's not a problem that the sky is pink. When the sky is pink in the morning, it is aesthetically beautiful. When the sky is pink in the morning, it makes you feel tranquil. When the sky is pink in the morning, it's a problem! Because you want to know why it's pink. The first thing to realize when you are solving a problem is that you are taking a mental model of the world and thinking of it from a problem-based perspective. This is important because it forces you to begin seeing the world as it really is, which includes your perception and all of its biases, for good or bad. The problem is not that the sky is pink. The problem is that you do not know why the sky is pink. But even that's not really the problem. The real problem is that there's a mismatch between what you know and what you want to know. What's fascinating is that when you use DSRP to identify the problem you will see that the not-problem is also the solution! So by using distinction making to identify the problem you have also identified what the solution looks like. We also can see the fundamental difference between the problem and the solution, which is the relationship caused by knowing or not. This reversal of identity and other, problem and solution, is a common structure. You'll see it exists in nearly any problem you try to solve. (See Figure 103.)

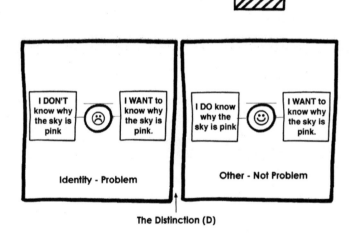

Figure 103

Index

General Assembly
  of IAU, 45
Gerry, E., 46–47, 47f
"gerrymander," 47, 48f
gerrymandering
  defined, 47
globalization, 124
Google, 122
Guardian, The, 47
guiding questions
  for distinctions, 33–34
  in part/whole structure, 73, 75
  for perspectives, 99–100
  for relationships, 79–86, 80f, 81f,
    84f–86f
  for systems, 59–60
  for universal structures, 27, 33–34
hand
  mind connection to, 121–22
Harris, P., 47
Harvard University, 128
Hawk, T., 11
hidden connections
  discovering, 80, 82–86, 84f–86f
  DSRP blocks in, 82
  DSRP diagrams in, 82
  tactile manipulatives in, 82
hidden perspectives, 100
hidden relationships, 80, 82–86, 84f–
    86f
higher-order thinking skills, 27
Hitler, A., 47
Hofstadter, D., 132
horizontal transfer, 20–21, 29
IAU. *see* International Astronomical
    Union (IAU)
identity(ies)
  in distinctions, 39–41, 39f
  lost, 42
  of relationships, 85–86, 86f
  from relationships with other, 42–45,
    43f, 44f
identity/other structure
  in distinctions, 39–41, 39f
Indiana University, 132
information
  defined, 4–5
  described, 3
  vs. knowledge, 22, 22f
information-full, 2–3
  vs. knowledgeable, 4, 4f
Ingram, J., 42

innovation
  algorithm for, 138–39, 138f
  methods for, 88–89
instructionism, 7–9
intelligence
  emotional, 2, 125
interaction
  in relationships, 78, 78f
interaction design, 89–90
interconnectedness, 124
interdisciplinarity
  interrelationships leading to, 86–88,
    87f
interdisciplinary thinking, 125
  defined, 2
International Astronomical Union (IAU)
  General Assembly of, 45
Internet
  invention of, 129, 131
  organization of, 135
interrelationships
  interdisciplinarity related to, 86–88,
    87f
Jeopardy, 3
Johns, J., 92–93, 92f
Jung, C., 77
Kahlo, F., 92, 92f
knowledge
  building new, 88–90
  content, 13, 125
  defined, 5
  DSRP Blocks of, 82, 120–22
  growth of, 10, 12
  relationships effects on, 86–88, 87f
  relevancy of, 11–12
  thinking and, 8
  universal structures in creating, 18–19
  validity of, 10–12
  vs. information, 22, 22f
"knowledge architects," 120
knowledge of universe
  in part/whole structure, 65–70, 65f,
    67f–69f
knowledgeable
  described, 4
  vs. information-full, 4, 4f
Ladins, 46
language
  distinction making preceding, 40–41
learning
  experiential, 27
  teaching and, 6

national standards for, 23–26
in part/whole structure, 75–76
thought
Eastern *vs.* Western styles of, 123
Time, 13
torture
distinction making related to, 51
transfer, 119
described, 20–21, 28–29
far, 28
horizontal, 20–21, 29
increased, 21
near, 28
vertical, 20–21, 29
21st-century education
DSRP Method applied to, 122–28, 126*f*
21st-century thinking
power of analogies for, 129–35, 130*f*,
131*f*, 133*f*, 135*f*
Tzu, S., 41
"under construction," 6–7, 7*f*
understanding, 116–19
increased, 21
unity
vs. quantity, 71–72, 71*f*
universal structures. *see also*
perspective(s); relationship(s);
system(s); *specific types, e.g.,*
distinction(s)
described, 18

distinctions, 31–56
DSRP diagrams for, 27
within DSRP Method, 27. *see also*
DSRP Method
guiding questions in, 27
metacognition-related, 129–35
perspectives, 97–112
relationships, 77–96
root list for, 27
systems, 57–76
universality
defined, 17
universe
knowledge of, 65–70, 65*f*, 67*f*–69*f*
in part/whole structure, 64, 64*f*
University of Venice, 103
Valerio, V., 103
130van der Waals, J.D, 46*n*
Van Gogh, V., 101, 101*f*
vertical transfer, 20–21, 29
view(s)
in perspective, 100–9, 100*f*
what something is by what it is not, 48
whole(s)
described, 61–63, 61*f*, 63*f*
organizing systems into, 70–76, 70*f*–75*f*
year(s)
distinction making in, 43–45, 43*f*, 44*f*